BEING THE CAUSE:
A User Guide to Responsible Living

By
Dr. G. Michael Durst

Published by

www.ArtofLivingResponsibly.com

Email: ResponsibleLife@aol.com

©Copyright by Dr. G. Michael Durst
2019

All rights reserved. No part of this book may be used or reproduced in any manner whatsoever without permission in writing.

978-0-578-22228-8

Front Cover Painting: "Entering a New Dimension" by G. M. Durst. Cover Design by Amilio Benjamin from Brandcology

Illustrations by Dick Sutphen: *Pen & Ink & Cross Hatch Styles of Early Illustrators* and *Attention Getting Old Engravings*, Hart Picture Archives, New York, NY

Forward for "Being the Cause"

It is an honour and with humility to provide the forward for "Being the Cause" by Dr. G. Michael Durst. This book represents the culmination of his lifetime experiences as psychologist, father, grandfather, husband, corporate human development professional and as an esteemed, world-renowned individual and artist. Dr. Durst is the "new" Carl Jung of the 21st century.

In this millennium, responsible healthy lifestyle choices are of utmost importance in improving our quality of life, preventing chronic diseases, such as obesity, diabetes, cancer, cardiovascular disease, anxiety and depression, and promoting graceful ageing.

Today, committing to and applying practical internal stress management, self-discovery and self-reflection tools and techniques, is as important as regular moderate cardiovascular exercise.

My observation as physician spanning over two decades is that a major cause for poorly managed, low-coherent stress responses in individuals, as well as in society, is the general inability to discern between the acceptance of our responsibility and accountability, rather than the choice of nurturing a blame/fault/guilt model.

The latter leads to relationships characterized by Drama, excessive and persistent adreno-cortisol responses, fuelling and aggravating inflammation, chronic disease and a general decline: physically, emotionally, mentally and spiritually.

Dr. Durst, eloquently, masterfully and coherently guides the reader with his wisdom, knowledge and experience in comprehending the discernment between being the "cause" in one's life, rather than being the "effect" of it, with its dysfunctional "they're doing it to me" attitude.

In doing so, he empowers individuals and groups to acknowledge that healthy relationships are loving, productive, highly coherent, co-creative and DRAMA FREE.

Unfortunately and sadly, victimhood with the unfolding drama, is still "gift wrapped" as a norm and our youth are deliberately misguided, confused and kept in the victim mindset, preventing them from attaining individual actualization in all aspects of their lives.

In my practice, (and for the continuous evolution of humanity), I recommend "Being the Cause" as essential educational, self-reflection, and growth material as part of a primary preventative treatment strategy.

Improved health outcomes are well documented in my practice as a result of applying and integrating Dr. Durst's philosophy. When engaging in lifestyle changes and choices, reading "Being the Cause" is an investment in your total well-being.

Dr. Durst's book will have a permanent place in your library, ALWAYS serving as a compass in managing your individual perceptions, your actions and your responses.

It will inspire and empower you, and the rest of humanity- to be the change catalyst for the world to move towards a loving, healthy, compassionate, kind, transparent, and co-creative 21st Century.

                                 -Dr. Casper B. Huisamen, MBChB,
                                 Cape Town, South Africa

BEING THE CAUSE
is about
YOU.

The purpose of this book is to allow you to experience more responsibility, satisfaction, and success in your life.

The book is written in free verse; it is not a book to "speed read." Reflect upon the words. Create your own sense of what they mean. "Fill in the blanks" with your own experience.

A Zen master begins his sessions by stating, "Imagine that I'm only talking directly and solely to you." Likewise, to gain maximum value, imagine that this book was written expressly for <u>you</u> because you are the cause in your life.

If you allow yourself to experience these words, you will create your own way. Your life will allow you to practice taking charge by being the cause and determining your own direction.

When education is meaningful it produces change. Simple awareness does not produce change. <u>You</u> produce change. Awareness only gives you a choice.

This book will best serve you by increasing your awareness, so that you may choose to change.

If this book only becomes one more in a series of "self-help" books, seminars, and lectures, it has failed its purpose.

If it assists you by increasing your self-knowledge and by expanding your options, it has succeeded in its mission.

BEING THE CAUSE is a culmination of my life experiences. As a therapist, teacher, speaker, administrator, and management trainer, I noticed one recurring theme:

Many people blame others and circumstances for their negative experiences.

And yet, it was the blaming that kept them stuck. Supporting such an "Effect" State ("They're doing it to me") only masked the symptoms of the underlying problem.

The problem was the unwillingness on the part of most people to take responsibility for their own experience. Eliminating one symptom simply led to the creation of another.

PLAYING LIFE FROM THE EFFECT STATE

When we say, "I don't like it," i.e. when we feel angry, upset, frustrated, embarrassed, or "put down," we often play from an Effect State.

We say, "<u>They</u> or <u>It</u> did it to me,"-- whether it was a spouse, a boss, the economy, the government or the weather. We tend to take no responsibility, and feel as though we had no choice in the matter.

I DON'T LIKE IT: THE EFFECT STATE

"They" or "It" Did It To Me - 0% Responsibility   No Choice

BEING THE CAUSE

However, when we say, "I liked it"--- whatever "it" was--, we play from a "Cause" Position.

"I did it to me" is generally what we acknowledge:
"I worked overtime to finish the project."
"I finished my degree."
"I have been working out."

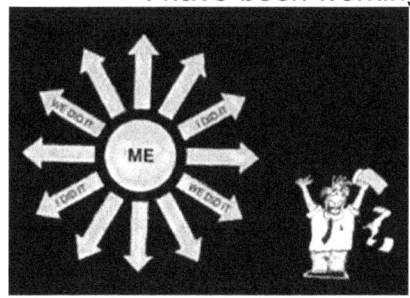

I LIKE IT: THE CAUSAL POSITION

"I" Did It To Me 100% Responsibility   Total Choice

If we like what is occurring in our experience, we tend to take total, 100% responsibility and we assume that we had total choice.

The truth is simple: we are responsible for everything in our experience, whether we like it or not. Liking or not liking the situation is only a matter of evaluation.

These same evaluations often change with time. Individuals typically report that what they deemed to be negative at the time- was, upon reflection, the "perfect" experience for them. (Have you ever gone back to a school reunion and experienced the relief that you DIDN'T marry that person?)

We've all been taught very successfully to play life from an Effect State, and to avoid responsibility. This book assumes just the opposite. Its very point of view runs counter to much of Western thought and its programming.

Indeed our very language is an "Effect" language. Listen to all the phrases: "You made me angry," "You hurt my feelings," "Time ran out," "She left me high and dry," "My boss frustrates the hell out of me." "The government is screwing us!" "My teachers are lousy."If you turn on the TV or go online you can hear and see dramatic examples of the Effect State. In fact, I have a friend who collects examples of what he calls "Country Western Effect Songs." These include:

"You Stole My heart and Stomped That Sucker Flat"

"You're the Reason Our Kids Are Ugly,"

"I Can't Get Over You Until You Get Out From Under Him"

and... "If This Ain't Thanksgivin', Why Am I Stuck With a Turkey Like You?"

Our society supports an effect position, both socially and politically.

The corollary problem is equally as devastating.

People often look to therapy, the government or religion to support and "save" them, which is the opposite of the Blame Game. In other words, instead of saying that something or someone is "doing it _to_ them," they wait for something or someone to "do it _for_ them."

People often wait for their therapist, mayor, senator, President, Prime Minister, professor, teacher, spouse, parents, minister, rabbi, guru or priest to "help" them or hope that some magical intervention will make their life work better.

Few heed Alan Watt's admonishment that if you see a signpost that says "New York," climbing the post won't get you to the Big Apple. Signs, like guides, can only point you in the right direction.

In order for any of your experiences to have meaning, one needs to assume the position of "cause." Otherwise, you're constantly searching for the latest, the best, the most wonderful "transformational" experience, and then feeling frustration because the impact doesn't last.

YOU are the one who makes your life work. YOU are the one who gets it all together, not someone or something else.

To assume that you're actually the cause of your experience goes to the root, the basis, the heart of the matter. To do so is to allow change to take place without "effort-ing", working at it, or _trying_ to make it happen.
Assuming a cause position enables you to take charge and to see the perfection of your experience.
It's as though you never escape the Truth you already know.

That's my experience. Aspects of the truth about how life works would become apparent in the strangest places at the strangest times.

This book was written on napkins, notes on to my cellphone and on my laptop in restaurants, on planes, and in meeting rooms all over the world. In fact, the original 1.0 version of this book was called, <u>Napkin Notes: On the Art of Living</u>.

When I was doing speeches and seminars all over the world, I would suddenly feel compelled to write an "Aha" or insight I experienced. Each time I would notice the simplicity and the beauty of the Truth.

Finally, the Truth all seemed so simple.

That's what the great philosophers and psychologists had been talking about for years! That's what Maslow's "self-actualized," Rogers' "fully-functioning," and Berne's "winners" were all about! That's what Christ, Buddha, and Lao Tzu meant!

Whenever I would find myself being the "effect" of my experience and living out the Drama, I would reluctantly have to acknowledge that I was the cause.

Once I made a note to myself:

*The Truth Is. You can't escape it.
Not because it's so good,
but because the Truth communicates Totally.
There you'll be forgetting that you're the Cause (or conveniently negating it), when all of a sudden
the Truth will seem overwhelming.
Making life work is like rowing with the current of the river; creating life not to work is like rowing up
stream. You might reach the same destination eventually, but OMG the price you have to pay!"*

Dear Reader-- it is my intention that these words will have meaning for you, and that they will assist you in experiencing the truth about
> *yourself-*
>> *your relationships-*
>>> *your job –*
>>>> *and your life.*

Many people know the science of living…which includes the mechanics of
> *how to succeed,*
>> *how to make money,*
>>> *how to gain status, and*
>>>> *how to handle the daily functions of life.*

Yet few seem to be aware of the Art of Being,
> *which is the ability to experience*
>> *the essence of what life has to offer*
>>> *and to hear the melody, not just the music.*

>> *My love and support in your journey,*

Dr. G. Michael Durst

"My task which I am trying to achieve is, by the power of the written word, to make you hear, to make you feel-it is, before all, to make you see.
That – and no more – and it is everything.

If I succeed, you shall find here… encouragement, consolation, fear, charm- all you demand-and, perhaps, also that glimpse of truth for which you have forgotten to ask."   -Joseph Conrad

Index

Searching for the Truth..p. 13

Being the Cause Means:

1. Staying Conscious...................................... p. 19

2. Being Where You Are By Choice...................p. 24

3. Living Life NOW...p. 31

4. Experiencing Your Aliveness.......................p. 37

5. Confronting Yourself..................................p. 53

6. Life Flowing, Expanding Your Beliefs, And Coming from the Truth................................p. 70

7. Giving Up the Drama and the Bad Feelings...p. 98

8. Satisfaction-Getting A Little.........................p. 135

9. Making and Keeping Agreements..................p. 153

10. Getting What You Want and Wanting What You Get..p. 170

11. Making Your Relationships Work....................p. 185

SEARCHING FOR THE TRUTH

Once a Truth-Seeker became frustrated. It seemed that no matter what
> discipline he studied,
> course he took,
> religion he followed, or
> book he read,

he just couldn't find THE TRUTH.

So he decided to take a trip
> to a place where lots of people
> are reported to know the Truth: India.

When he arrived, the Seeker looked for a Guru.
(Guru's are people who know what the Truth is.)

He asked everyone the name of India's Top Notch, Holiest, Numero Uno, Number One, Primo Guru.

After weeks of searching, the seeker came upon an Ashram. (An Ashram is where Gurus hang out.)

The large sign in front said:

"The Guru is in, please take a number."

The Truth-Seeker was led to a room where he waited and waited… and waited.

Finally, the Guru appeared.

He was a little guy with a big smile on his face.
(You always smile when you know what the Truth is)

"How can I serve you?" asked the Guru.

"Master, I have traveled a great distance. I've tried so many ways to find the Truth. Do you know what the Truth is?"

"Of course, I know what the Truth is.
How could I be a Guru if I didn't know the Truth?"

"Sorry," said the Seeker, a bit embarrassed.

"Would you share the Truth with me?"

The Guru looked at the Seeker intently.

"It's just not that easy. Living is an Art.

To know the Truth, you'll have to pay the price."

The Seeker gulped. Of course there would be a price.

You don't' get something for nothing!
A Guru would have to be out of his mind to give the Truth away for free.

The Seeker, gathering courage, asked: "How much money will it take?"

The Guru laughed. "The Truth doesn't cost money.

The price is that you'll have to perform a service for ten years. The task you are to perform is obvious."

The Seeker, who had been a disciple and a follower before, knew the story. "I'll do whatever is necessary, Master."

"Good," said the Guru as he pointed.

"Do you see those barns down there?"

Indeed, the Seeker could not only see the barns,
He could *smell* the barns.

"Those barns are the dwelling place of the Sacred Cows.

In order for you to know the Truth, You'll have to keep those barns spotless for ten years,

When you have performed the task, come back and I'll share the Truth with you."

The Seeker thought about what the Guru had said,

"Ten years…… *Ten years* ! ! !"

There was no way he wanted to shovel cow dung for ten years, sacred or not!

No way!

But as he pondered, it became obvious by the way the Guru smiled that the Guru knew something that he didn't know.

If he could just figure out THE TRUTH his life would work.

Like the Guru. he could have that same Satisfaction and Inner Peace,

And that would be worth any price.

"O.K., I'll do it!" The Seeker shouted triumphantly.

He began his task. Days became weeks, weeks became months, months became years.

The Seeker at times seemed like a robot.

He even forgot for long periods why he was shoveling.

He seemed to be doing it just for the sake of doing it.

Finally, the last day came.

At sunset, he ran up to the hill to the Ashram where he had stood ten years earlier.

The Guru looked as though he had been expecting him.

Out of breath and stumbling, the Truth-Seeker shouted,

"Master, I've done it. I've done it.

I've cleaned the dwelling place of the Sacred Cows for ten years.

Now, will you tell me the Truth?"

The Guru smiled. "Yes, my son. You've worked so hard and you've kept your word. Now you can know THE TRUTH:

The Truth is YOU ARE."

The Seeker said, "Yes, go on. I'm ready."

The Guru looked at the Seeker and simply stated:

"That's it. That's the only Truth there is.

The Truth is YOU ARE.

You've spent your life asking that question and the last ten years discovering the answer."

Realizing that was the extent of the message,

The Seeker stopped.

The combination of
　　　anger,
　　　　　fear,
　　　　　　　humiliation,
　　　　　　　　　and disappointment
　　　　　　　　　　　showed in his voice.

"I don't get it! I shoveled and shoveled for ten years to find out:

　　　　　　　I AM!

　　　　　I just don't get it."

The Guru just smiled and asked,

 "How much more

are you going to have to shovel before you do get it?"

1. BEING THE CAUSE means STAYING CONSCIOUS

The Truth is, "You are." It's been around for thousands of years.

Great philosophers,
    religious leaders,
        sages and
            prophets have told us.

They've all told us, and we've refused to listen.

The only
Truth in the universe
is "You Are."

That's it.

Few want to accept the answer.
Few want to see it that way.

Most of us want to hold on to our illusions:
> that someone else knows the real Truth;
>> or
> that we have to study for years to find it;
>> or
> that only the wisest can know the Truth;
>> or
> that only the wisest even care.

The Truth is:
> Your Experience is your Reality.
> Your Reality is your Experience.

Your experience of the universe flows through you.

No one else
> is experiencing what you're experiencing,
>> or what you have experienced,
>>> or what you will experience.

From where you're sitting right now, there is only one truth in the universe and that Truth comes when you say,

> "I am."

That's all you can say, because that's all you know, and that's all you'll ever know.

(You *are* totally certain that you EXIST, aren't you"?)

Of course:

"These truths we hold to be self-evident."

But you're not so certain
> that anyone else really exists,
>> or anything else for that matter.

(Maybe there's no one else out there.
Maybe life is just a damn good virtual movie.)

We go on thinking that the world exists independently
      and we're independent of "it" or "them."

If you think the world is "real" and independent
from you, (the source), ask yourself how you would prove
that "they" exist.

Once you've proved it – notice the person to whom
                you proved it.

The wake-world reality of
sensory perceptions are only your
experience…

They don't *prove* anything…

Anymore than a rose proves
anything…

A rose just is.

Your sensory perceptions are simply
your sensory perceptions.

Maybe you made up your sensory
perceptions like you made up the rest of your universe.

You don't know that this book is "really" on your screen or
in your hands, now do you?

All you know is that you're having a sensory perception of
it. You can see it and touch it.

But maybe it's just another prop in the virtual movie
you're creating, called "This is your life."
And a damn good virtual reality experience it is!

You've been playing your role so well
	you even had yourself convinced.

Marvelous performance! Bravo!

You've written such a convincing
	plot that it even fooled you:
			the programmer,
			the source code,
			the writer,
			the main character,
			the director,
			the set designer,
			the choreographer,
			the make-up artist,
			the stunt man,
			the camera man.

You're not only **in** the virtual movie, you're also **experiencing** it.

Your experience always comes back to you.

When you look beyond your act, to your essence,
	all you know is that you are.

And there's no way to prove it. And no need to.

You are	I am
because	because
you are	I am.

Nothing could even have taken place until you said,
	"I am."

How would you know that you had done something, if you weren't aware that you were?

"You" wouldn't have been there for it because
"You" wouldn't have existed

To exist is to participate with the awareness of self:

I AM

therefore I think, not vice-versa,
therefore I feel, not vice-versa,
therefore I sense, not vice-versa.

To say,
        "I KNOW I AM"
                is redundant.

Being-ness just makes the statement: I AM.

And it's only verifiable to you.

It's the best-kept secret in the universe.

It's the first,
    last,
        and only provable statement in the universe
            to you.

And that's the only person to whom you could prove, it because

        The Truth
          is
        You Are.

2. BEING THE CAUSE means BEING WHERE YOU ARE BY CHOICE

Once you know you are,
then, you have to ask,
"So, where am I?"

> YOU ARE…
> HERE.

The strange thing about being "here"
is that it's very possible to <u>not</u> be here.

You can be two places at once.

(While reading these words, your mind may be wandering...for example, you may be thinking about the fact that your car needs to be fixed.)

Let's say the last time you had the car repaired, you became angry because you felt you had been overcharged.

Through your mind's recall mechanism you can relive the entire experience.

To find out where "here" is,
imagine that a piece of the ceiling above your head, just

        fell
              right
                      now,

        while you were mentally re-experiencing
        the scene in the mechanic's garage.

Where would you feel it?

Where you are sitting right now, or in the mechanic's garage?

"Here" is defined by your physical presence.

"Here" is where your body is.

We know we're here, because this is where it's all taking place.

When the ceiling falls you get to have a lump on your head here where you are reading these words – not where your mind was.

That's one of the problems with being in two places at once. It's dangerous!

When your mind abandons your body, it can put both in jeopardy.

It's called being unconscious.

BEING UNCONSCIOUS CAN BE DANGEROUS!

You can get your "token" taken away very easily!

In Monopoly, your "token" is a top hat, a Scotty dog, or a car. In life, your token is your body. Take your token away and the game is over. Get badly injured and you lost your turn.

Even if you don't lose a turn, your body can get pretty scarred. That's what happens in a universe that's filled with ceilings that fall.

Most accidents happen because "Nobody's Home" mentally. Your mind goes on vacation and leaves your body to baby-sit. Sometimes you even become "Lost in Space or in the Cloud" for that matter, and that's when it's really dangerous.

Ever get into your car and drive to your destination and not be able to remember driving there?

You don't remember, because your mind was "Out to Lunch."

That's usually when you get traffic tickets. The cop is like a Cosmic Custodian reminding you to stay conscious when you drive.

The reason you can't remember the drive was because you weren't there for it. And now with Self Drives you can really go unconscious but at least the AI stays conscious and aware…no wonder it will be safer!

The truth is if you're not "here" for the experience of life you can do disastrous things to yourself and others.

What's worse is that when danger does occur, your mind always seems to want to "leave the scene of the accident."

You enter an unconscious state, which even further immobilizes you.

You become like an ostrich – the mascot of unconsciousness.

Whenever an ostrich is frightened or bored, it puts its head in one place and its body in another. It likes to stick its head in the sand, where it's warm and comfortable.

But notice when you stick your head in the sand, you put yourself in the ultimate vulnerable position.

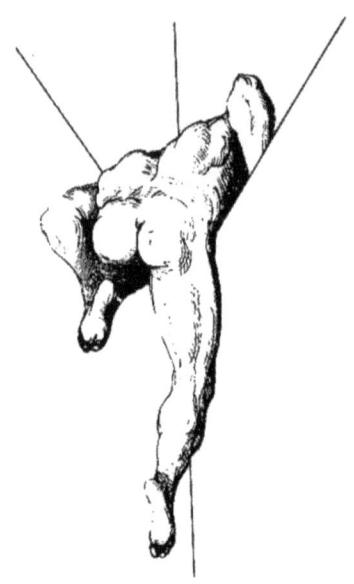

(That's your ass hangin' out there in the breeze!)

And you keep wondering why you're getting kicked?

People, circumstances, and events keep shouting

"Wake up, wake up, wake up!"

It's dangerous when your mind splits—
and that's just one of the   problems…

When you're unconscious, communication with another human being is difficult, if not impossible.

When you think about the times you had difficulty communicating with others--when they just didn't seem to 'hear' what you had to say or when you didn't hear what they had to say –

it was because one or both of you were unconscious…

Your minds were somewhere else.

Maybe you were thinking about something else or rehearsing what you were going to say or the person said something that triggered an association, and vice versa.

That's why most conversations are a one-way dialogue, rather than a two-way communication process.

Ever had a spouse or friend or boss report that they gave you an important bit of information-such as:

>Going over to Jim and Sue's place,
>>Making certain that the email went out on time or
>>>Forgetting to pick up something from the store,
>>>>and…
>>>>>you didn't remember?

(Of course. You probably weren't *there* for the communication.)

Besides being dangerous
　and creating a real communication problem,
　　being "Unc", (unconscious), can make producing
　　　results
　　　　very
　　　　　time-consuming.

A lot of people are paid for eight hours of work –
　　for which they're "there" for about two.
　　(and that's usually lunch and breaks!)

Ever read the same paragraph fourteen times?

Spent an hour writing a short blog?

Taken a twenty-minute shower?

Uploaded a few photos for what seemed to be hours?

It's difficult to perform a task when you're really not there for it. You can miss a lot if you're not there for it.

Strangely though, life continues.

       Experiences pass us by.

   You bought the ticket, but didn't get onto the bus.

     LIFE is a "Be There For It" proposition.

    You might find less danger,

        fewer accidents,

        deeper communication,

        more results

        and greater satisfaction

    if you decide to participate in your own life.

    Participation does not mean analyzing
                or
           projecting.

    It means <u>experiencing</u> what's there
                        consciously
                                  right Now.

3. BEING THE CAUSE
means
LIVING <u>NOW</u>

The eternal instant is Now.

>The only time you can be
>HERE
>is
>NOW.

Now is all there is. It doesn't last any time
at all.
It just is.
It exists outside of something called
"Time."

Time is just a convenient recording mechanism.

Your mind has several filing systems. One method of retrieval from your mental hard drive is "Chronological order".

That's all for the mind's Systems Department.

It has nothing to do with what's happening.
You have never experienced anything, except NOW.

Your mind records an event and categorizes it, sequencing it into seconds, minutes, hours, weeks, months, and years. It uses the concept of time to place the data on its own storage platforms.

It generally conceptualizes it all as

    Past   Present   and   Future.

The past consists of all the data of experiences that is stored on the drive and commonly known as "Memories".

The future is the mind's ability to anticipate and create data that has not yet happened.

Usually we think of NOW as the present and that's true.

It's also true that NOW was the past and will be the future.

Look at it:

When you were two years old, what time was it?   NOW!

And when you were sixteen, what time was it?   NOW!

And when you were twenty-two, what time was it? NOW!

It's always been right   NOW!

And when tomorrow comes, what time will it be?
NOW!

The future can only exist in now, and the instant it does, it's not future. Future is simply a mind projection.

Now is all you have. It's all you've ever had.
And it's all you ever will have.

Get the joke:

  When is the time to clean up your life?

  When is the time to make your relationship work?

  When is the time to produce results?

  When is the time to make those changes you want?

  When is the time to start that project?

There is only NOW.

In that NOW you can produce a result, tangible or intangible.

> You have the choice:
> You can either produce a
> result
> or
> you can prevent a result from being produced.

A result can be produced when your mind and your body are united. When your mind is not functioning with your body, it may be impossible to produce a result.

Not that your memory data storage isn't useful in producing results. It is. In fact, those memory data tapes are necessary for survival.

You don't have to be constantly hit by cars or burn your hand on a stove to notice it hurts. You can recall the memory tape of the original incident and learn from it. We learn physically from our past tapes.

Yet we neglect the same process that constantly saves our lives. We should look at our past tapes as incidents from which we need to learn.

In other words, we need to ask what is the lesson to be learned from that divorce, illness, accident or dismissal rather that spending all of our time justifying our actions, complaining about it, blaming others or being "right" about the past event.

It's like constantly burning your hand on a stove, and complaining because the stove shouldn't be there. Maybe, someday, you'll learn not to put your hand on top of the burner or to move the stove!

If you don't like an event in your life, look at it and learn from it.

If you do like the event, recall what you did to set it up – and repeat the process.

The mind and all its storage systems can be the master or the servant.

It can search to shift cause and moan about negative experiences or it can assist you along your journey.

The mind is the series of recordings actual, imagined, exaggerated, erased, or created, by the mind itself. It's a never-ending cycle.

The mind not only records past events, it also projects future events. The future doesn't exist. The past doesn't exist. Only NOW exists.

You are indeed eternal.

What does your experience of past tell you?
How far back can you go?
Can you recall a time when you weren't?
Can you accurately remember when you didn't exist?

Your experience is that you've always existed.

From where you are right now, you don't know whether your parents created you or you created your parents.

Notice how funny it is to moan about what your parents did <u>to</u> you or are still doing to you!

And from your perspective, you can't think of what it would be like not to exist. You'll never know.

What matters is that there is only one
time in which you can exist. That one time is NOW.

You may decide to use your mind
    to learn from the past and to plan for the
        future
         or
to complain about the past and to worry about
       the future.

It's up to you. It's your life or non-life. Have any choice?

The truth is you already chose. You're here aren't you? You <u>are</u> reading this, aren't you?

To BE, HERE, NOW is to be conscious.

To be conscious is to have your mind and body united in the same time-space frame.
To become Consciously Conscious –
    to be more alive,
        to live life artfully, -
            may be a difficult game to play.

What you may have to do is confront that which you don't want to confront.

Consciousness is not a game that you "should," "ought," or "must" play. You already are.

It's a game you might <u>choose</u> to play consciously to increase your satisfaction.

You are the only one
    who can determine your own satisfaction.

This book, your loved ones, friends, teachers, parents, therapy, seminars, or the government won't do it for you.

You're going to play or not as *you* see fit, when *you* see fit.

That's the way it works.

It's your choice to Be Here Now or not…to be the cause or the effect. It's totally up to you.

The Truth is You Are.

So why not be Here for the experience of what's happening Now?

Why not experience your life, rather than simply going through the motions or the process?

4. BEING THE CAUSE means EXPERIENCING YOUR ALIVENESS

Who Are You Really, and How Did You Get To Be That Way?

In order to get in touch with who you are *really*, we have to acknowledge how you became that way in the first place.

It all began with Creation.

Once upon a moment of NOW you were conceived.
    (Hopefully it was fun for someone!)
There you were... something from nothing.

Being and changing.

Totally supported by the world's greatest life support system:

MOTHER!

And she created a comfortable growth environment:

There was no bright light.
The temperature was accurately controlled at 98.6 degrees.

The life-support tube carried oxygen and disposed of poisonous gas,
        (no breathing

        no coughing

        no gasping for air)

   supplied food that was already digested,
        (no eating
        no hunger
        no acid-indigestion)

   carried away food wastes,
        (no elimination
        no constipation
        no diarrhea).

And you were weightless, comfortably floating in your own little heated pool.

No need to exert yourself.

Nowhere to go.

You started your taping sessions… Recording it all.
 No considerations, evaluations, guilt, embarrassment, worry.
      Just direct and straight recording.

But gradually, you began to feel a bit crowded.

You were out-growing your space. ("If one more person moves into this neighborhood...")

One day, after about nine months, the walls started to press on you. Then they stopped.

Mom started to get a bit upset.
    Her heart was beating faster and faster.
        She seemed to be gasping for air.

You felt your heart pounding,
    "Hey, what's happening?"

    Then *WHOOSH*!

"Wait minute, who's draining my swimming pool?"

The walls started squeezing you
    tighter and tighter
    faster and faster.

All of a sudden you felt real whoozy, so dizzy you could hardly stay there for the experience.

You could feel your head being squeezed through a small tunnel:

"It's too small. I'll never fit. No way. My head's too..."

The ultimate pain subsided with a clear slide into

    LIGHT!!!

"Oh, my God! It hurts... It's too bright!"

And it was so
    COLD!!!
It had always been 98.6 degrees.
Now you were freezing your ol' wazoo off!

And then there was all that noise. The talking. The clinking of instruments.

Someone's finger probed your mouth, and drops were added to your eyes.

Finally you were picked up by the heels and

>SLAPPED!

>Welcome to the Western World!

You began to shake from your own sound and your own fear. "Oh God, this is awful. Lord forgive them, they know not what they do!"

And THEN: They cut the life-support tube!

Instant death!

Cut off from all of life's process.
No food, no waste removal, no oxygen.

NOW you were on your OWN.

Now you had to start scratching for your very SURVIVAL.

And that's birth:
The first time you learned *NOT* to BE HERE NOW.

In order to survive the

>fear,

>pain,

>and suffering,

You created a mechanism that allowed you
a mental escape valve: AT&T: AIN'T THERE THEN.

Your mind split to another time– space scene
where it was more comfortable.

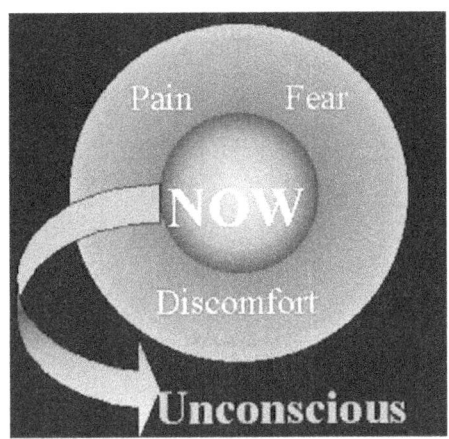

A. T. & T. (Ain't There and Then) = Unconsciousness

At that point you went back to your tapes of the womb,
where the reality of your survival needs didn't exist.

The same process continues now. Your mind splits when
you feel threatened or uncomfortable.
You go unconscious.

When threatened, your mind creates a
place that doesn't exist--
                      Fantasy Land,--
where there is no hostility or the discomfort
of the "real" world.

Splitting is very functional. Deep within you
knew at birth
that if you stayed in such a painful, hostile
universe too long
       you'd go crazy or die.
So, you chose the next best thing:

To go crazy in stages.

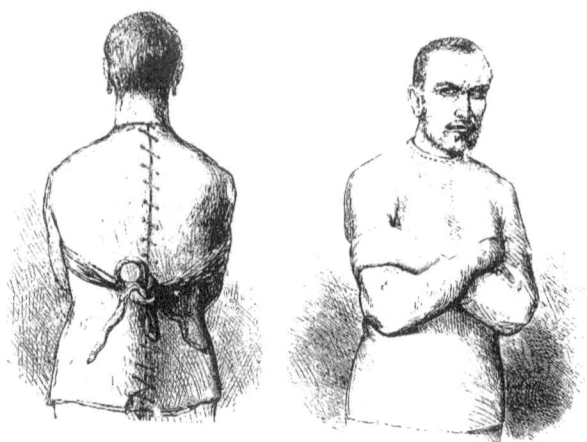

With each split, a new neurological path is formed.
    An association is made.
Events become symbols and triggers for more and more splits.

Eventually almost anything could trigger an escape
    into Fantasy Land.

At some point, you become more <u>un</u>conscious than conscious. Your mind takes over: it dominates because survival is an important persuader.

In order to survive, your mind records everything you've ever experienced. It's like a computer that stores all the tapes on its data base using an information retrieval system. When you want information, your mind looks through the tapes to pull out the appropriate data.

The purpose of the stored information is
    to provide the knowledge of "How To Survive."

The storage contains
    memories, concepts, beliefs, and associations.

Paradoxically, even though the purpose of the tapes is survival, some of the responses and associations are so inappropriate that the body is put in jeopardy.

The Cosmic Joke is that the mind is so intent on survival that it will sacrifice the body to insure that the tapes will survive.

The all-important tapes are in chronological order and cross-referenced by subject and tied together through associations.

Graphically, your mind would look like this:

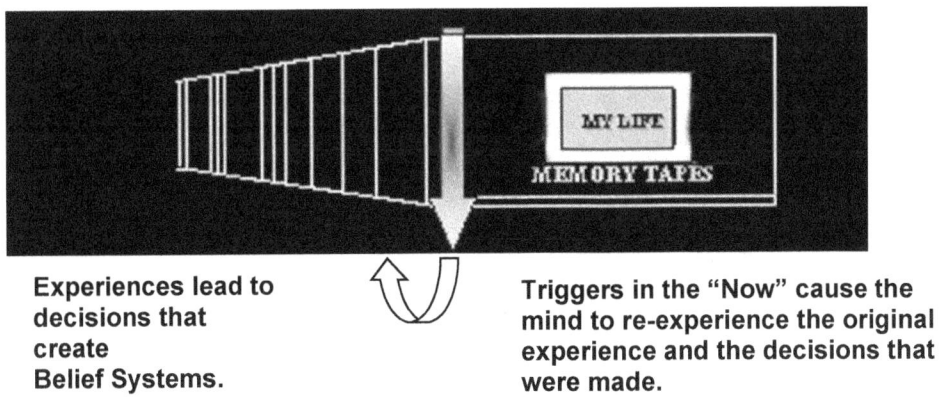

Experiences lead to decisions that create Belief Systems.

Triggers in the "Now" cause the mind to re-experience the original experience and the decisions that were made.

Anytime your mind desires, it can split from NOW, go into the past, and play any old tape.

And since the trauma of birth, you've let your mind split whenever it chose. It's as though you said to your mind:

"OK" you saved my life, now you can split anytime you choose."

There's only one flaw:

>Your mind is often an absolute idiot!
>>Sometimes it pulls out the wrong data.

Sometimes the past response is inappropriate for the experience of NOW.

Often the mind gets stuck in a particular response and wants to play it over and over.

Eventually there are a lot of recurring themes:

Look at the times you're angry;
>at the times you're frustrated;
>>at the times you're embarrassed;
>>>at the times you're hurt.

Notice the patterns and the triggers.

Don't you always have the same fight with your spouse?

When was the last time you said,
"Hey, honey, let's fight about something new tonight!"

Not too original in our behavior patterns, are we?

These automatic patterns begin to act as barriers.
  Barriers keep us from experiencing the world,
  and the world from experiencing us.

The walls we built to keep others out are also keeping us in.

The strongest automatic patterns are related to our primal needs. If we don't satisfy these needs, we die. Primal patterns provide instinctive behavior to insure our survival.

The next level of automatic patterns is triggered by a set of symbolic needs. A symbol is a representation that stands for something it isn't.

$ is a symbol for a dollar. It is not actually a dollar. It won't buy anything at the Dollar Store! You cannot satisfy your needs, psychologically, through symbols. You may think of possessions as symbols of security, and yet you may have all of the possessions in the world and not have security.

Some of us use food as a symbol of love and approval:
  ("Good kids finish everything on their plates.")

Others as a symbol for the elimination of physical pain:
("Oh, you fell down. Come inside, I'll give you a cookie.")

Or as a symbol for the elimination of psychological pain: ("They won't let me play we them!" "OK. Well, we'll have an ice cream cone then.")

Symbolic behavior can be a little crazy: When you're happy, celebrating, and feeling loved, <u>you eat</u>.

When you're sad because you look unattractive and feel rejected, <u>you eat</u>.

Then, when you feel guilty for having eaten too much, <u>you eat</u>.

That's how much of an idiot your mind can be. And how ridiculous such patterned behavior can become when you inappropriately respond to triggers from the past.

BEING BOUND TO YOUR PAST

The more automatic responses you have, the more your vision is restricted and you can't see what's really going on.

Since all that's necessary for an automatic reaction is a stimulus, life becomes a knee jerk reaction – a mental reflex.

Even events that are similar will run an old tape, evoking the same archaic feelings:

> Someone gives you constructive criticism
> and you respond defensively...
>
> -Just like you did with your father years ago.
>
> A friend or loved one forgets to call, email or text, and you feel, "No one really loves me,"
>
>   -Just like you did when you were a child.

When you ask someone who is programmed who they are, they will tell you what they did yesterday.

We become like robots, machines, and computers or even like
> a 1950's Wurlitzer Juke Box!

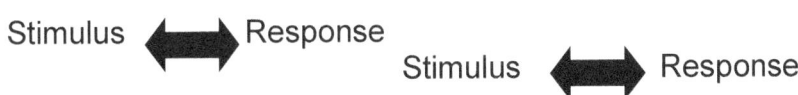

We become like a Wurlitzer Juke Box.

> A Wurlitzer is not a very happy person.

Its "records" are stacks of tapes, recorded by the mind.

You push its buttons for a replay of a particular tape
> to get the kind of "music" you want.

For example:

Your spouse might push your A-11 button –"Why did you spend so much money? You know we can't afford it."

You then immediately bring out your tape to defend your position.

We become machines by running out our numbers,
    which become our automatic behavior patterns.

The Wurlitzer seeks to develop new programs to defend itself from every possible contingency.

And in order for it to work, it has to be "plugged in."

This is a pretty grim view of humanity:
   Stimulus-Response Being Machines.
  It can become depressing.
        There is very little aliveness.

And yet, it seems as though you can't step outside of this reality anymore than you can step outside of yourself.

We push each other's buttons, without even trying.

Notice how easily we "plug into" anger, upset, and hurt.

Once you slip into "Out of Control," you've really gone unconscious.

Because of our button-pushing expertise,
the name of the game in most relationships is
     "I'll push yours – You push mine."

Being a Wurlitzer is bad news.

THE GOOD NEWS

The good news is once you admit how mechanical and how programmed you are, you can start to live more of the essence of who you *really* are: the Cause of it all.

Then you can be more alive.

Unlike the Wurlitzer, you can reach down and unplug the device. You can defuse your own mechanical responses.

Of course, you may have to shovel some more smelly stuff before you can comprehend that
      you're the cause
    of what's going on
        and
    before life starts to work
      for you.

And that's totally OK,
      because at least
        now you know
            and now you know
                that you know.

Remember –
> Life seldom works out for people who
> don't know what's going on.

Automatic behavior patterns often act as barriers –
> barriers that need to be transcended.

Yet when you're right up against a barrier, life can become real uncomfortable.

Often the more uncomfortable it feels, the closer you are to a solution.

And that's the area of your life that is taking away most of your aliveness right now.

THAT WHICH YOU FEAR CONFRONTING THE MOST, SHOULD BE WHAT YOU CONFRONT FIRST!

The instant you push beyond the barrier,
you'll notice what whatever you were afraid of
> vanished,
> evaporated,
> went poof!
> Just like that!

One of the problems, however,
   is that your mind always thinks it's silly,
      or it's too much work,
         or it's too inconvenient,
           or it's not appropriate right now,
              or it's too complicated,
                 to make life work for you.

When you're up against the barrier, clarity is right there on the other side. That's what comes next. The light at the end of the tunnel is there –you just have to open your eyes.

When you confront a barrier, you realize that it was a phantom.

It was a product of your own imagination. It will disappear in a cloud of smoke, and you'll ask yourself, "Why was I afraid of that?"

What good does it do you to fear something, except as a signal that you'd better take action now?

Fear can take away your aliveness right now.

FEAR can take many forms:

Embarrassment
> is the fear of exposure and of having people find out that you are actually the person you always feared you were.

Anger
> is based on the fear that you might be wrong,
> or that you might not be listened to,
> or that people won't give you respect,
> or that you're not alright the way you are.

Hurt
> is a fear that someone doesn't love you,
> or appreciate you,
> or that they may share the same low opinion of you that you hold of yourself.

To break some of your automatic behavior patterns and live your life responsibly you will have to face your fears.

5. BEING THE CAUSE means CONFRONTING YOURSELF

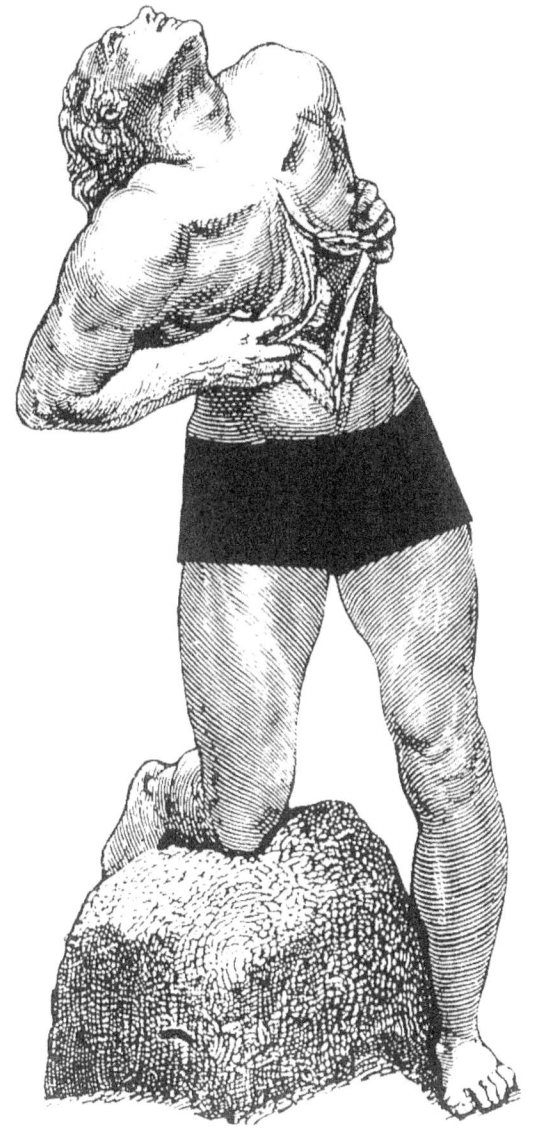

Life is a series of problem-solving exercises.

Since you can always add new tapes, it may seem like a never-ending, boring game.

People who are totally in their tapes don't see a way out.

The way out is to play exactly the same way, but to notice that there's a possibility that you are alive while doing so.

To do that, dissipate some of your
       automatic behavior patterns.

Take a look at one of your problems right now.

1. WHAT ARE THE TRIGGERS?

2. WHAT DO YOU GET OUT OF HAVING IT BE THAT WAY?

3. WHAT'S THE PATTERN?

4. WHO GETS TO BE RIGHT?

5. TELL THE TRUTH ABOUT IT ALL

And

6. KISS IT ALL GOOD-BYE.

What you'll experience is a rush of energy, a new lease on life, more spontaneity, and another increment of aliveness. To rid yourself of a problem –

Stop looking at it as a problem. It's an
opportunity
to be alive.

You have to stop making it wrong to have problems.

The only people without problems are those who are
six
feet
under.

(And we're not too sure about them.
They're just harder to interview.)

To be more alive
you need to face
your problems.

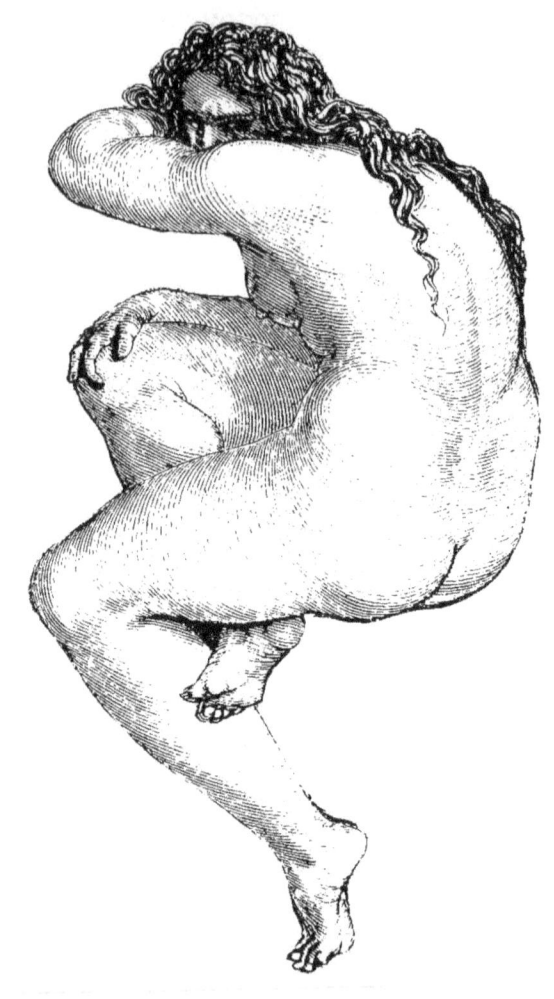

**Remember:
   whatever you're afraid to face
  will always
       bite you in the ass.**

1. What are the Triggers?

You'll only be able to play
"Locate the Trigger"
when you're conscious.

You can't do it when
you're in the middle
of a taped response.

You have to wait until you're
back in the Here and Now.

After you've run your number –
      thrown your tantrum,
      had the same old fight,
      plugged into your boss –
      <u>then</u> you can ask:

"What was happening just before I went
      unconscious?"

Your triggers need to be examined.

In many cases, the original experiences
have been associated with so many
    other symbols,
    that it all becomes
    non-sense.

As you know, many people would rather
save their
    Mercedes
        than their own Ass.

The triggers may have become so symbolic
that whenever anyone even mentions
    money, sex, politics, or
    gets the least bit close to you –
        you go unconscious.

A funny thing happens when you become conscious of the trigger: You begin to dissipate some of the energy,
    the moment you look at it.

The more energy you release from that tape.
the more freedom you will feel, and the more
        "authentic self"
    you will experience.

It takes a lot of time and energy to build and to maintain negative self-defeating responses.

And these responses keep you from experiencing
    who you are and who you can become.

The negative energy that is on the tape
    makes your mind want to flee the scene
    whenever it gets close to anything remotely
    associated.

Yet putting your hand over your eyes
    doesn't make the world go away.

You're still experiencing your experience
    whether you want to look at it or not.

When you begin to examine triggers
that start automatic behavior patterns,
initially you may think –"It doesn't work"
because you're still experiencing the same old Drama.

At first you may only shorten the cycle by maybe a minute or even a second.

The second time you look at the trigger, the automatic taped response may be a little bit shorter.

Sometimes you will be unable to detect the difference
    Until all of a sudden, you say –
  "God, something like that used to get me so plugged in and upset and this time I hardly noticed it!"

"YOU SPENT <u>HOW MUCH</u> FOR THAT DRESS?!!"

If you simply care enough about yourself
    and the people you love, to persist
in confronting those negative taped responses,
    you'll start seeing and feeling, the results.
      And so will they.
You won't go out "there" quite so far
        or
    stay quite so long.
      You'll experience less unconsciousness.

When you first start to dissipate the energy that was bound to the past and start to use it Now, you may start to feel High.

That's how it feels to confront something really difficult and win.

It's a good feeling to know that you'll again have all the energy that was tied up in the tape.

You can use it however you choose:
    to heal yourself,
    to be more productive,
    to be more loving,
    to become conscious of
        your own life.

Locate the trigger so you can notice the tape, so you can confront the issue, and so you can experience more aliveness.

2. What Do You Get Out Of Having It Be That Way?

The second part of the game – after you've played, "Locate the Trigger," is "Determine the Payoff."

The tapes and the automatic behavior responses exist to serve a purpose.

Your payoff may be
> to defend yourself against the fear,
> to make someone else wrong,
> to protect your incredible ego,
> to have something to moan about.

To determine your payoff you have to look at what you get out of having the situation that way.

Your problem may be your ability.
For example:
> Your problem with _____X_____
> may be your ability to get people
> to feel sorry for you.

YOUR PROBLEMS MAY BE YOUR ABILITY TO GET OTHERS TO FEEL SORRY FOR YOU

Having a lousy relationship at least gives you
something to talk about –
just no satisfaction.

You're the only one
who knows the payoff
for you.

Asking someone else what *you*
get out of the situation
is like asking someone else
to have an orgasm for you!

Locate the trigger and tell the truth about it.

Face what you get out of having it be that way.

3. What Are the Patterns Involved?

When you determine your payoff,
you'll notice recurring themes…

For instance:
If you always had incompetent supervisors, maybe your payoff was that you were able to make them wrong.
    (*They* were always the SOB's!)
  Maybe you were able to tell others
    what a rotten boss you had.
Maybe you were able to make your boss
    responsible for your mediocre performance.
Maybe you were able to re-experience the same familiar
    experience you had with your parents.

Or

If your spouse always spent too much money,
    Maybe your payoff was that you got to be
        right about the need for money.
    Maybe you were able to feel like the only
        responsible party.
    Maybe you were able to play some old tapes
        that you heard as a child.

What you're beginning to realize is how many patterns you have. Some take a few minutes. Some take a few weeks. Some take relationships to fulfill.
    Some take a lifetime.

Perhaps the same things that are causing you problems on your current job, are the same things that caused your problems on your last job,
    and the one before that,
        and the one before that,
            and the one before that.

Perhaps
    what's causing problems in this relationship
    may be the same factors that caused problems
        in your last relationship.

Until you're willing to face it, the old theme will always be there.

So taking the position of Cause, makes it worth the time and effort to determine the patterns
      so you can end the cycle.

4. Who Gets To Be Right?

You created the patterns to get something out of them and now you need to tell the truth about that, too.

Many of us set up automatic behavior responses to get out of responsibility…to play life from the Effect State.

As long as you can make
your boss
your spouse,
your secretary,
your kids
or
your parents
      wrong-
you don't have to take responsibility for results

or

the lack of results.

If you persist in looking at your payoff, honestly, to see
what you get out of having it be that way –
it always seems to have something to do with
getting out of your own fundamental
responsibility in that matter.

You get to be right…and alone.

5.Tell The Truth About It All

Stop lying about who
created your problems.

To guarantee that you get
stuck on a problem
blame someone else for it.

When you stop putting
energy into blaming
    other people,
        circumstances,
            and events
for what's going on in your
life, you're on your way.

You created your own
tapes and automatic
responses.

And you're holding them in
a place with your own
energy.

Whatever the problem is –

if you keep running from it,

if you keep turning your back on it,

if you keep going faster to avoid it,

    it'll still be right behind you.

You become like a dog chasing its own tail.

Wake up to the fact – that it's all you.

When you begin to tell the truth about your taped responses

    when you've paid your dues,

    when you've shoveled enough cow dung,

then you'll notice a geometric progression
    into awareness.

The mechanism of an automatic behavior response

    cannot stand the focus

    of your consciousness

and cannot maintain itself when you acknowledge that you are the cause and you need to take responsibility for it.

A demolition expert
> knows where to put the charges
> to blow the building sky-high.

You must demolish your taped responses
  and only you know where to put the
> dynamite.

After you've blown up the automatic response you may hear echoes or reverberations. A trigger will hit you and you'll go
> -zip-
  in and out
> and back again.

You'll start to realize that the automatic behavior mechanism is faulty. It just won't run all the way out there
> like it used to.

You'll just say, "Oh, yeah, good ol' number E-7,
> I remember that one!"

Your old numbers will sound as empty as echoes.

You'll sit and stare at that
which had always triggered
you into unconsciousness
and it won't work
anymore.

You'll just start to let things
    be the way they are
    and that's
       when life begins to
       flow.

SUMMARY

Of course, you can still plug in whenever you want.
All you have to say is
        "I'm not responsible."

Your old number will come up
      and you'll be able to run it out as
         long as you want.
But then, that's what got you into this mess in the first
place.

The good news
  is that you don't have to be on "automatic pilot,"
      you don't have to be a Wurlitzer.
      You can do something about it.
      You're the only one who can.

And...I already know that
    you already know
      everything
      that I know
    and that you've been avoiding
        acknowledging it.

Because that would mean
> that you've *been* responsible for your past experience,
> that you *are* responsible for what you're experiencing now,
> that you *will be* responsible for your experience in the future.

To avoid taking the responsibility,
you've been playing dumb.

> (Now that's really dumb,
>> because the joke's on you.)

Avoidance doesn't change the truth
> or
> the way it is.

With jokes like that, here's hoping you have a good sense of humor.

6. BEING THE CAUSE means EXPANDING YOUR BELIFS AND COMING FROM THE TRUTH.

I've Got Some Bad News,
And Some Good News!

The Bad News
    is that you're a Wurlitzer
    with tapes from the past,
    with automatic behavior responses,
    with buttons that can be pushed anytime.
    And the more automatic you are
    the less you know it and
    the less you're willing to admit it.

The Good News is
        you're not just a Wurlitzer.

A tube?   You're also a tube!

Well, what does the most self-actualized, fully-functioning Guru do when he gets up in the morning?

(He empties his tube just like you do.)

Isn't life exciting? Every morning you get up and empty your tube.

Then fill your tube with breakfast,
    putting it into your input hole.

Then you go to work,
    drink some coffee – and fill your tube.

At break, you empty your tube
    so you can fill it up again.

At lunch – guess what?
    You fill your tube, then empty it
    before you go back to work.

At your afternoon break, you empty
    your tube and fill it with a snack.

Finally it's quitting time and you can hardly wait to fill your tube at dinner. After dinner, you watch TV or go on the internet and periodically fill and empty your tube.

Before you go to bed you empty your tube again,
so the next day you can start the same
             exciting
                     process all over again.

The only reason
   you have arms and legs is
      to get you from the refrigerator to the john!

If you wanted to eliminate the middle man –
      you'd put the refrigerator in the john!

Once you realize how much of your life is spent in carrying out pre-programmed responses and in filling and emptying your tube – you have to ask –

What am I doing here?

What's the purpose?

Why am I experiencing life?

The age-old question. The simple answer:

We are here experiencing life so that we might *experience* life.

   Not just the peaks,
      but also the valleys.
   Not just the highs,
      but also the lows.

You're here to experience all of it.
And what do we all want out of our experience of life?

Satisfaction.

Out of each experience in your life what you really want is satisfaction.

    It's the bottom line.

You're not working for money,
    you're working for the satisfaction
    you hope that the job and money can bring.

You're not in the relationship
    for any other reason
    than the satisfaction it can produce.

All there is in the universe is experience.

You are an experience-tube.

You are a vehicle through which the experience of life passes.

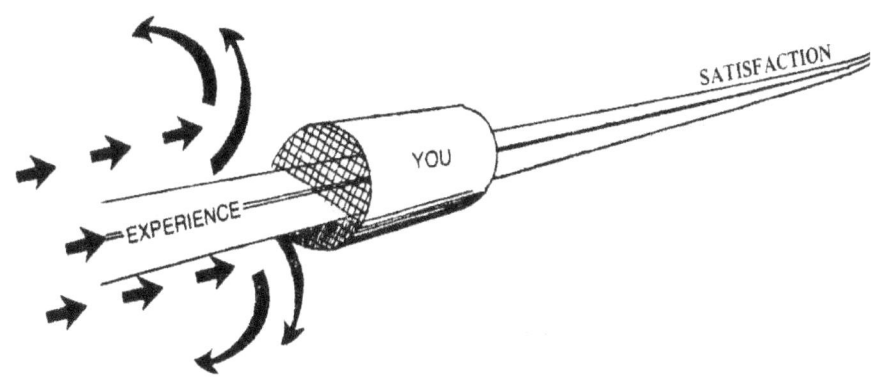

The Tube

The problem is you've got a screen in front of your tube that blocks out much of the experience that life has to offer.

It keeps you from a large part of you.

The screen is made up of your beliefs about your reality.

The beliefs that restrict your view of reality are those
    that you've made totally
        right,
            reasonable,
    logical,
            justified,
                and
                    provable.

You look at all your potential experiences and you make judgments about whether they are
    good or bad,
        right or wrong,
             moral or immoral,
                crazy or sane.

And somewhere in the back of your mind, is the truth:
    that they are, "None of the Above."

        They just are.

What takes place in front of your tube
        is
            the Experience of Life.

The Experience either flows through the tube or
　　it hits the screen and flows around you.

　　　(And you never know it.)

It's like being a wallflower,
　　saying, "Look at all those people having fun!"
There you sit wishing, hoping or just wondering
　　　　"What the hell is going on?"
　　　WHY NOT COME TO THE PARTY?

When you don't allow the experience of life to flow
　　through you, you become a wallflower.

It's happening all around you and you've protected yourself
from that which you desperately need to make life
meaningful and satisfying.

The beliefs that keep you from experiencing are the same
ones that shape the fabric of your universe.

They are a product of your education, your upbringing, your parents, and your society…everything that has gone into making
    You be
    the you that you are.

You've built this screen that tells you

    what kinds of experiences you can have,

    what's good and bad,

    what status you should achieve,

    what kind of   job/house/spouse/car/children
        you should have,

    how much money you should make,

    who would make the "right" kinds of friends,

    who would make the right type of spouse.

And if anything doesn't fit your belief of how it should be,
    you just don't experience it.   (That'll show it!)

Whatever you believe, you see as the truth
  and it either is, or it becomes that way for you.

Christ knew that and attempted to share it with the Apostles,
> but had a difficult time of it
> because they had not yet experienced it.

It's not something you can just tell someone.

Your belief systems
> insulate you
> from
> everything that doesn't
> agree with them.

(They keep you from having the experience of non-agreement.)

Your belief systems will even use science, (which is itself an organized system of beliefs about the universe),
> to prove the belief
>> … and it does.

(That is, until the agreement in the scientific world shifts.)

Every great scientist had to transcend
        the then current set of beliefs
and gain consensus from peers
    that his or her new beliefs were better.

Our egos are so large

and
      our minds are so strong,

        that even when we find an exception to our belief,

    we use it to prove the rule,

        rather than disprove the rule.

For instance, prejudice is simply series of
      particular beliefs focused
      negatively on a particular group.

These aspects are considered to be inherent within each member of that group.
Let's say that you have a belief that:

men-

your relatives-

Mexicans-

union members-

African Americans-

Italians-

executives-

Puerto Ricans-

poor people-

Gay people-

government workers-

women-

rich people-

children these days-

people on welfare-

teenagers-

teachers-

Irish-

Mid-managers

        are "lazy."

Then you notice that the person down the street is a member of that group, but works his ol' wazoo off.

What your mind says is, "Sure, so and so works hard, but then [he or she] is the exception, because everyone knows that all ___x___ are lazy."

For example, even to this day, some executives still secretly hold the belief that women make poor managers because they are too emotional.

They say, "Jane is a great manager. She's not too emotional. But she's the exception.

Because, as everyone knows, women can't make rational decisions because they're too emotional."

And then they promote one of the male applicants.

Sound familiar?

SOMETIMES THERE ARE BARRIERS TO CONFRONT

**REMEMBER...YOU
CREATE
YOUR
OWN
REALITY
BECAUSE
YOU ARE THE
CAUSE**

You hold certain beliefs about reality, which create your
reality, and then, you smugly say:
> "I told you so."
> or
> "Sure Enough!"

Your beliefs
> totally manifest themselves
> and that has little to do with logic.

Your beliefs may be limiting
> the experience of what life has to offer.

Once you transcend
> your beliefs,
>> you'll find yourself in a very
>>> different world.

Your belief systems about
> love
>> often limit the individuals with whom you can
>>> experience love.

Look at all the considerations you have about-

sex,
age,
body-types,
hair,
eyes,
lips,
breasts,
cars,
weight,
education,
interests,
voice,
money,
clothes,
teeth,
acne, etc., etc.

These considerations limit your sources for love,
(much less sex.)

Life is not a discard.

It's an all
      inclusive reality where
        the more you accept
          the more you get.

Some of our basic beliefs are no longer relevant.

The most potent ones come from early childhood
when you lived at home with the "Giants" called "Mom" and
"Dad" who did "magic" like prepare food, drive cars, open
doors, get you drinks of water, and make you feel better
when you were sick.

They were so powerful. And you seemed clumsy, weak,
noisy, and bothersome.

Knowing that your very survival depended on them,
 you made what they had to say "significant."
It was as though they had the power to tell you what was going to happen to you forever.

However, some of what the Giants said was ridiculous, insane and inappropriate. Perhaps you heard:

"You're lazy"

"You can't do anything right"

"You'll never amount to anything"

"You're stupid"

"You drive me crazy"

"You're a clumsy ox"

"You never finish anything"

 "You just can't be trusted"

  "You're a big cry baby"

  "You're too sensitive"

  "You never listen"

   ... and you believed it!!

This may be a shock to you but....
 you're not two years old anymore!
Your parents never had magical
 powers to cause you to be anything you didn't
  choose to be.

You may not be that way at all. All you have is NOW.

You're the one who decides who you are and what's right for you NOW.

You can't even blame your parents and make them responsible.

That's a great game
and total B.S.

In large families parents can give each child the same message.
> Some accept it.
> Some reject it.

We're right back to *you* being the cause of your experience.

Your beliefs about who you are and what you can become are imposed limitations that you've made reasonable.

The only difference between you and the CEO of the company is that the CEO has given himself or herself permission to be "CEO" and you haven't.

Millionaires have transcended their beliefs that they couldn't be millionaires.

(Notice the results.)

Take a look at some of our society's beliefs:

"Have fun now, kid, because when you get into the cold, hard, cruel world, it won't be any picnic."

"Live it up, because when you get married, it'll be different."

"Just wait until the kids come."

"If anything can go wrong, it will."

"You can't trust anybody."

"Give a person an inch and he'll take a mile."

"If you want something done right, you have to do it yourself."

We unconsciously follow our beliefs and make them right.

A young woman who has a belief that

"Men are only after one thing…"

may be unconsciously flirting.

So every time a man makes a pass at her, it proves, "Mom was right."

Rightness and proof can keep you stuck.

You selectively perceive what you want to perceive.

Drive down a busy street:
    if you're hungry, you'll see restaurants.
        if you want a drink, you'll see bars.
            if you're low on fuel, you'll see filling stations.

When you change your perception of yourself,
  the people, circumstances, and events also change.

Wouldn't it be nice to take off your blinders and see what's really out there?

Wouldn't it be great to see yourself as the person you really are?

Many people are more afraid of success, than they are of failure.

To be successful, would be to go against the beliefs acquired earlier in childhood. It's scary to be on stage, when you've just been handed a new script.

The old one may have been a real bum act, but at least you knew your part and you knew how it was going to end.

No one ever told you that if your life has become a soap opera,
            a melodrama
                or
                    a tragedy
that you can change it,
        or you can walk off the stage.

Someone told you that was the way it was- and the way it had to stay. You believed them and you've been making them right ever since.

It's time to come from your own experience, rather than your beliefs or someone else's beliefs.

Complete the following:
I am _____
because _____

Now list all the "because's."

The "because's" are the beliefs standing in the way of change.

The word itself says it all:

be cause: **"Be" the "Cause."**

Beliefs keep us stuck and they're the mechanism with which we keep others stuck. Often the belief systems have to do with what you "can't" do.

The word "can't" often means "won't."

Every time you say "I can't" you justify why you aren't.

You don't have to defend what's happening right now.
The universe is what it is.
Judgments and interpretations about the way it is,
     rob you of your experience of it.

Remember, it's your beliefs which act as a grid in front of your tube limiting your experience.

Even though you have a screen, some of your
    life experience flows through your tube and
        you experience what life has to offer.

Other experiences, however, get stuck in your tube.

That which gets stuck are all the
        lies you've told.

You know what you can do and what your abilities are.

Every time you say "I want that" and you don't take
responsibility to get it – it gets stuck in your tube.

All of your unrealized goals and unfinished projects-
      get stuck in your tube.

The new car you said you wanted to have
    and you don't have it?
        That's stuck in your tube.

The degree you said you wanted
    and don't have?
        That's stuck in your tube.

That weight you said you were going
    to lose and haven't?
        That's stuck in your tube.

The promotion you were in line for
    and you didn't get?
        That's stuck in your tube.

That perfect mate you have fantasized about
    and you still haven't met?
        That's stuck in your tube as well.

A Human Being Suffering from a Terrible Disease:

COSMIC CONSTIPATION!!!

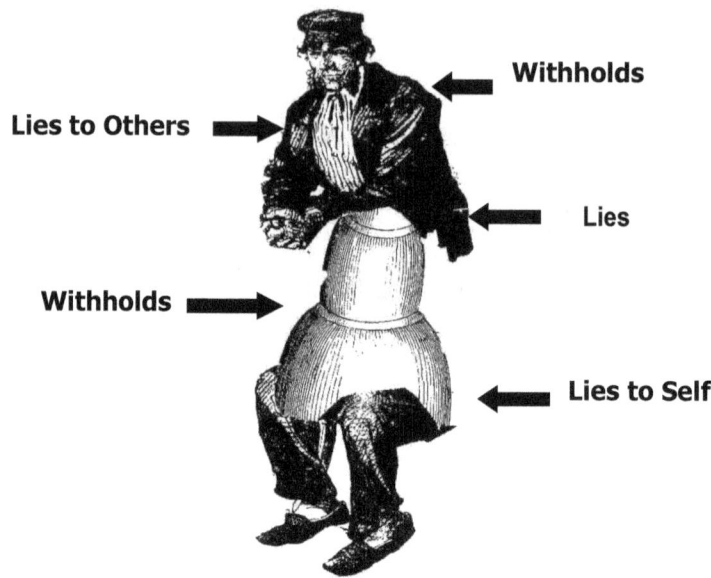

Your tube gets clogged. You've become solid as a rock. Nothing can pass.

Everything you've said you wanted and don't have,
is stuck.
Everything you've said you wanted to stop and haven't,
is stuck.

Everything you've said you wanted to start and haven't,
is stuck.

These are all lies you told to yourself.

Pretty soon you get Cosmic Constipation.
When you're constipated what do you think about all day?

You constantly re-experience your failures
because they often are manifestations of lies.

The blockage keeps you from being able to choose
> a new goal.

The tube keeps getting more and more constipated.

Many people get to the point where they
give up. They tire of all the strain.

Do you know anyone with Cosmic Constipation?

Take a look at the person who's sitting in the chair that
> you're sitting in right now.

No wonder life doesn't flow for you!

How could it?

You've become stuck in so many ways, in so many areas
of your life, you've begun to feel a bit sluggish.

These lies are not sins that will cause you to go to Hell
when it's all over.
> You won't have to wait.

When you lie, it *is* Hell. You Unc out every time. Your lies
drive you crazy. You always pay yourself back for the lies
you tell.

And the lies you tell yourself are the real fundamental
> rip-offs –

Get the joke:

> "I think I'll lie to the only person who
> always knows the truth about my experience:
>
> > Me."

What do you think constant lying does to your gut?

If you're ill,
        depressed or otherwise in pain –
clean out your tube – clean up your life
        and see how you feel.

Withholds are vicious because you always pay yourself back.
You don't have the same satisfaction with that person.

Communications won't flow easily.
You won't feel good.

    A LIE IS A BURDEN WE CARRY
        AROUND WITH US

You have two and only two options
    to clean out your tube:

Number One: JUST DO IT.
If you have unrealized goals stuck in your tube, you'll have to complete them, so your life will start to flow again.

Number Two: TELL THE TRUTH ABOUT IT.

You didn't want it anyway.

Now, ain't that a kick in the kimono?

Think of all the dues you had to pay to get it stuck in the first place! Look at all the rationalizations, reasonableness, excuses and rightness that you've used to justify not completing the action.

To get your life to flow you'd have to give up all that B.S.

        Shame.

Not only do the lies you tell yourself
    get stuck in your tube
    but so do the
        lies you tell others.

Your lies to others are in two forms:
    Blatant Lies:
("Honey, sorry I have to work late tonight…")
    And
    Withholds.

Withholds are the truth recognized but not communicated.
  ("What they don't know, won't hurt them.")

(Hell no – it won't hurt them – but it might kill you!)

Don't kid yourself: lies and withholds create a
        physiological response.

That's how a lie-detector test works.

Some of our most significant
    withholds are positive.

You don't share with your spouse/parents/kids/friends/co-workers
    how much you love them,

        how much you appreciate what they do,

        how much they mean to you.

What are you waiting for?

A catastrophe?

An illness?

A quit?

A divorce?

A death?

Grief is often a function of a loved one dying with
    lies and withholds.
  "Oh, if I had only told them how much I cared…"
        Why not do it NOW?

Your lies and withholds have been keeping you from truly experiencing that other person.

If your relationship isn't working, it's because of the
    lies and withholds.
No technique, no therapy, no "special" week-end, no book
    will help until you've taken the responsibility of
        cleaning up your relationships.

Lies and withholds and satisfaction
    cannot occupy the same space.

Lies take away your aliveness,
> your consciousness, and your satisfaction.

> That's quite a price to pay.

The more lies within an organization, the less satisfaction for the people who work there.

The more lies within a family,
> the less love experienced.

The more lies within a classroom,
> the less growth and learning that take place.

The more lies between us,
> the less we communicate.

Your life works to the extent that you're willing to tell the truth about how you set it up.

"The truth shall set you free."
> (What do you think He was talking about?)

And you always
> know the truth
>> about your lies.

You can't kid yourself because you always know the results. You can always prove that you didn't want the goal you said you wanted.

> If you don't have it – that's all
>> the proof you need.

If there's no energy on the lie, you don't have to mess with it anymore.

If there's still energy – if it's still bothering you –
> you'd better handle it.

You're the only one who knows, and the only one paying the bill.

It's like the expression from the Old West,

"You've got to separate the BS from the gun smoke."

The truth is:
Life is satisfaction/love/ results. Or the BS as to why it isn't.

It's D.D.S.--
    Dog Doo Simple:

You've either stepped in it

    or you haven't,

and you know right away.

You either have satisfaction or lies.

You're either loving life or moaning about it.

You're either expanding or contracting. There ain't any middle ground, no grey – It's on or off. There's no other way to play it..

To make life work-
    to get more aliveness
        to become more conscious,
            to make your relationships work…

Tell the truth about who gets to be right;
    about your payoffs,
        about your patterns, and decisions;
            about your automatic behavior responses.

Then take 100% responsibility for your experience now.

Stop blaming other people, circumstances or events.

Start being who you are – a loving, ethical being
dedicated to producing satisfaction
                            for yourself and others.

Share with others
  so you can be around people who
      are alive,
           loving,
                and kind.

And then just
        sit back
            and enjoy
                the party.

Now that *is* the Good News!

7. BEING THE CAUSE means GIVING UP THE DRAMA AND THE BAD FEELINGS

If It's My Party, Who Are These Other People?

If the only truth in the universe is
"I AM"
then who are these other people in my experience?

You just can't be too sure.

>Maybe there's no one else out there!

>Maybe they're all just a part of your virtual reality!

>Maybe they're just other avatars.

But one thing is for certain.
What you see in others is simply your own reflection.

When you look at someone else you're looking into a mirror.

It's as though that great-cosmic-part of you didn't like playing alone so it went "poof"
and created another part of you to play with,
and you lied about that, too.

You said the other was a "not-self"
>a "someone else"
>a "not me"

You said the other had "nothing-to-do-with-me".

Take a look in the mirror again. "Mirror, mirror, on the wall, who is the who of us all?"
>"I am."

All beings are a reflection of you.

And you're a reflection of all beings.
Love thy neighbor as thy self.

"In everything, do to others as you would have them do to you; for this is the law and the prophets."
Jesus, Matthew 7:12

"This is the sum of duty: Do naught unto others which would cause you pain if done to you."
Hinduism – Mahabharata: 5, 1517

"Hurt not others in ways that you yourself would find hurtful." The Buddha, Udana – Varga: 5, 18

"Surely it is the maxim of loving –kindness: Do not unto others that you would not have them do unto you."
Confucianism – Analects: 15,23

"Not one of you truly believes until you wish for others what you wish for yourself."
Islam –The Prophet Muhammad, Hadith

"Lay not on any soul a load that you would not wish to be laid upon you, and desire not for anyone the things you would not desire for yourself. "
Baha'i Faith, Baha'u'llah Gleanings

"What is hateful to you, do not to your fellowmen. That is the entire Law; all the rest is commentary."
Judaism – Talmud: Shabbat, 31a

Every religion promotes "The Golden Rule" because all religions have been teaching aspects of the Truth
or
they wouldn't have survived.

Notice the statement "Love thy enemies…"

Of course, you need to love your enemies as well as your friends. They're also part of you.

Perhaps they're

    that part that you fear,

    that you don't like about yourself,

    that you refuse to accept in you,

    that you don't want anyone to know about,
        including yourself.

If you don't like what you see
    in others
take a good hard look
    at yourself.

    Mirrors don't lie.

When you start to accept yourself
    the way you are,
you'll allow others more freedom
    to be the way they are.

When you focus on aspects of yourself
    that you don't like,
you continually create those same aspects in others
    until they are resolved within you.

Once you're able to allow the other people to be who they are and realize that you are the "cause" of your relationship with them, then you can stop moaning about the fact that people are exactly the way they are.

Then maybe you can start to
    communicate with them.

The strange thing is
we're all out to change...the other guy:

Parents want to change their kids.

   Kids want to change their parents.

Husbands want to change their wives
   and vice-versa.

Teachers want to change their students
   and vice-versa.

Managers want to change their employees
   and vice-versa.

Public officials want to change people
   and vice-versa.

    The *cause*
        is
            you.

Be the way you want your kids to be.

Act the way you want your spouse/teacher/boss/employee/ to act.

   And stand back and watch what happens.

If you want to change someone else –start with you.

The other person's behavior is simply a reflection of your beliefs and behavior.

Aren't your kids terrible when you've had a bad day?

Don't your employees use the same excuses you
   give yourself?

Don't you customers give you your own objections?

Your experience of others is a result of
> your intention, conscious or unconscious.

When you like what you see in others,
> you acknowledge your reflection.

When you don't like what you see,
> you say, "That's not my
> intention!"

Really?
Whose intention is it?

Is God punishing you?

Did the Devil make you do it?

Are the Martians directing your actions?

Is someone else sitting in your chair?

Is someone else paying your bill?

Notice that if you resolve the problem
from your side
there's no problem.

No solution requires two people.

Two people pushing against one other create stress through resistance.

If one stops pushing, there's only flow.

It takes two
> to tango
> to make war
> to argue.

It takes one
> to solve the problem and
> *to stop the aggression.*

War is a "no-win/no-win" situation.

Psychological games are also "no-win/no-win."

To play from "I lose/you win" – is a loss.

To play from "I win/you lose" – is a loss.

Why lose?
Why do we set up "no-win" situations?
Why would we have negative experiences?
Why, if you're a reflection of me, do we have to go through all this?

It's very simple: to be **Dramatic.**

We continually lie to ourselves and others
> to make our lives dramatic.

>> The greatest lie in the universe is:
>> "I'm not responsible for my experience."

> (Who put you there?)

> (Who's going to have to get you out of it?)

When you play life from a position of "no responsibility" you can play a wonderful role called "The Victim."

Victims take no responsibility by definition – that's what makes them Victims. In order for there to be a Victim there has to be a Persecutor. If there's a Persecutor around, you can bet there's a Rescuer.

Steve Karpman says those three roles,
       Victim, Persecutor, Rescuer,
          provide all the Drama in our lives.

The Dramatic action comes from switching roles on the Drama Triangle:

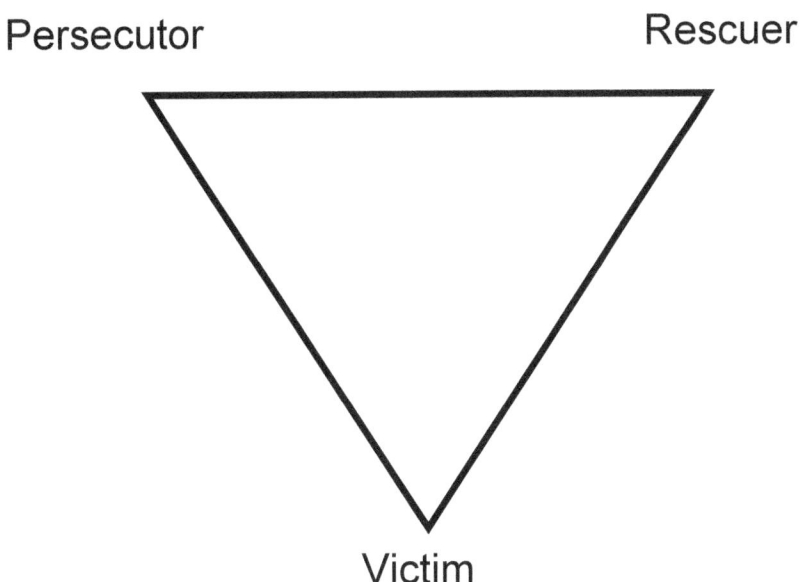

The Drama Triangle

PERSECUTOR, RESCUER, VICTIM

The Classic Story

John Jones can hardly wait to get home from work to tell his wife how his boss has been persecuting him all day.
        Poor Victim.

Jane Jones can hardly wait till John comes home so she can tell him how the kids have been persecuting her all day.
        Poor Victim.

The Jones kids are awaiting the arrival of their father, John, because mother has been telling them all day,
 "Just wait until the persecutor comes home. He'll punish you."
        Poor Victims.

Enter Victim John, greeted by Victim Jane, who immediately reports her plight.

Victim John turns into Rescuer John, in order to help his damsel in distress, and yet feels victimized saying to himself,
        "Aw crap, now I've got to play Persecutor, when I wanted to play Victim."

Angrily he stomps into the kid's room – and
"lets them have it."

Rescuer Jane hears their pleas, and enters just in the nick of time to rescue the kids and to persecute John for being so mean.

Victim John stomps out of the house and goes to the bar, hoping to find someone to "understand" (Rescue) him.

Tune in tomorrow, folks, for another exciting episode of "As the Stomach Turns."

Those three roles create lots of Drama –just no Satisfaction.

Satisfaction only comes from the truth.

All three positions are based on lies:

Victims always try to get out of their responsibility. They take 0% responsibility.

Rescuers try to "help" victims by taking responsibility for them.
That's 200% responsibility.

Persecutors try to force the victim to do something and feel that if it weren't for them, nothing would happen.
They also play it from a 200% position.

Playing life from a 0% responsibility or 200% responsibility is a lie.

We all have 100% responsibility for our experience.

There are no helpless Victims in the Universe.

Victims always want to convince you that they had no responsibility in the matter.

Let's say you're standing at a four-way intersection. And you're about to be the star of Victim Productions.

You look and the light turns green and says, "Walk."

So you know you're doing the "right thing."

Then you go unconscious, not noticing
> the bus that just ran the red light
> and it flattens your little ol' body in the middle of
> the intersection.

What good does it do for you to yell

"I had the right of way""
"He ran the red light"
"I'm the helpless victim"

Who has the flattened body?
Who is dead right?
Who has to pay the bill for your experience?

Even if your body isn't totally flattened –if you just became a double-amputee in a wheel chair –
what good would it do to blame the bus driver for the rest of your life for what he did to you?

Notice your experience always comes back to you. You're the one who did everything necessary to produce the result.

That was _you_ who chose to be in that city at that time, wasn't it?

It was _you_ who chose to go down that street, wasn't it?

It was _you_ who took every step necessary to
    get your body flattened, wasn't it?

It's totally OK for you to cry:
    "He ran the red light!"
    "I'm the injured party!"
    "Why does it always happen to me!"
    "It's their fault!"

Notice, however, that you've already paid the bill.

You paid it. And you didn't like paying it.

Now you're making it worse by moaning/groaning/feeling sorry for yourself/and playing right/wrong.

And it's a reaction to being ticked off about the bill.
    (Sorry)

Take a look at how effectively your
    cries,
    moans,
    and groans
        change the event.

(Doesn't work too well, does it?)

Taking total responsibility seems to come in stages.

Stage One:

At least take 100% responsibility for your <u>reaction</u> to the event. in other words, notice it's **Response-Ability**.

You can live the rest of your life
> a cripple, feeling "un-faired" against,
> being victimized,
> or
> you can be productive, happy, and successful.

> You have total choice and total responsibility.

100 % Responsibility for Your Reaction to the Event

100% Responsibility for Putting Yourself in a Position to Experience the Event

PERHAPS IT'S REALLY RESPONSE-ABILITY

You are totally responsible for your reaction to each event. After each event reflect upon it:

- Has that event or a similar event occurred before?
- Is there a pattern?
- What do the patterns have to do with your belief systems?

- What might you be doing to set up the situation?

- What can you do to avoid negative events in the future?

- Whose responsibility is it to react in a positive manner, learn from the experience and change negative patterns?

>Notice it all comes back to you.

Stage Two:

Once you start taking 100% responsibility for your reaction to the event, you'll start to notice that you're responsible for the event itself.

You're the one who created yourself in the space where the event occurred. Take a look and see if it has anything to do with your belief systems.
> Review your tapes and see if similar events have occurred in your experience before.
> Let yourself get back to the original experience.
>> Re-experience the tape, but
>>> this time by telling the truth about it.

You may notice certain patterns, decisions, or belief systems about which you get to be right.

There's no way out of taking responsibility for your experience. If you aren't responsible, who is?

> God?
> The Government?
> The President?
> Your Parents?
> Your Company?
> Your Boss?

The only way to escape the fact of your responsibility is to "unc" out. The problem is, if you wave your ass in the breeze someone's bound to give you a close shave. You can't get out of responsibility because you're the one with the bald ass.

The fact that you're totally responsible for your own fate doesn't negate a Higher Source. In fact, the more responsibility you take, the more you *experience* the reality of that Higher Source.

You were given freedom of choice –then you negated choice, then you negated responsibility.

Taking total responsibility and thus being the cause of your experience is a tough concept because everyone has been telling you for so long, that you're not responsible; that you are the effect of your experience. But take a look at all the choices inherent in any given situation:

Look at all the things that had to happen for you to be reading these words. Who has to take ultimate responsibility for it?

(Does somebody have a gun in your back forcing you to read?) You had to set it up carefully to be here right now, just like I did to be here with you with these words. Clever aren't we?

Who's responsible to translate these concepts into meaningful behavior changes to make your life flow smoothly?

Tell me that I'm responsible and I'll just laugh and laugh – because I don't even know you.

In any situation, why not ask yourself:

What you're getting out of this experience?

What are your physical sensations?

When have you experienced those feelings before?

What do they tell you about yourself?

What emotions are you experiencing?

Are these emotions ones that you experience often?

When did you make the decision that these would be your "favorite" emotions?

What do your emotions tell you about you?

What attitudes do you have about yourself?

What do you feel about the other people included in this event?

Are there any patterns?

What lesson should you learn from this?

Look at the event; experience your "Aha's" and insights and then do everything necessary to change the event. Learn from it –then go on.

Certain people seem to have the same, (or similar), events reoccur, often.

>   Some people can never find a parking space.

>   Some people are always in trouble.

>   Some people always have bad marriages.

>   Some people always have tyrannical bosses.

Just coincidence? Sounds like a lot of shoveling.

No coincidence.   No magic.   No luck.

If you ask yourself "HOW" you created the event in your experience, it may take you years to study quantum physics, to get a sense of thought/energy transformation and bio-gravitational, self-organizing, field forces,

> and then your mind would probably reject it all anyway.

If you ask yourself "WHY"
> you created the event in your experience you may

> a.) never figure it out,

> b.) not know for years, the significant pieces of the puzzle called your life,

> c.) catch a terrible disease called "Paralysis by Analysis"
> (i.e. through analyzing your life, you may stop living it and experiencing it. You may become totally mentally paralyzed.)

Take a look at it:
If you get killed in an "accident" it may not have been your "fault," however, you are definitely responsible for being dead.

At that point, it becomes a null program.

It doesn't make any difference who is at "fault" or to "blame."

It's like saying: "Wait a minute! I'm not dead!"

Except you can't say that when you're dead. Or maybe you can, but no one will hear you.

If you want to play the game of life to experience satisfaction you need to assume that you're the cause of your experience.

To gain more satisfaction you have to give up your Victim role.

Everybody loves to indulge themselves in the fantasy called,
> "Someone or Something is making me unhappy."

The truth is that an instant of NOW went by and you *chose* to be unhappy. That's the way it works. There's no one kicking you in the ass to make you unhappy.

You do it to you. You've always done it to yourself.

Without Victims, there are no Persecutors.

Some Victims choose to be persecuted
> just to avoid responsibility.

That's when the Rescuers enter the drama.

> Rescuers take responsibility for the Victim.

> Rescuers create and maintain others in Victim positions.

> So Rescuers can feel good about themselves.

> So Rescuers can feel superior.

> So Rescuers can assuage guilt feelings.

> So Rescuers can feel their life is meaningful.

Rescuers victimize the very people they say they're helping.

Rescuers rob Victims of the opportunity of getting in
>touch with what they've done to themselves.

The rest of the story is that Victims end up resenting the people who rescue them.

If you're a Rescuer,
stand back,
because
the Victim you
>save today
>may Persecute
>you tomorrow.

In the United States, we come from a nation of Rescuers.

We've never understood why all those
>undeveloped nations we rescued, ended up
>resenting us.
We can't understand why our welfare programs
>foster resentment for the very government that
>>provides them.

We wonder why kids
>don't take responsibility; and
>why they end up persecuting us
>>later.

You only *serve* people
>by getting them in
touch with their
total responsibility
in the matter.

That's called treating
people with Dignity.

It's nice to let Victims in on the
Facts of Life:

>Do you know what
happens if you don't get
what you want?

>Nothing.

Do you know who cares about that?

>Nobody...
>>except you.

Once you become aware that nobody cares whether you get what you want out of life, you'll begin to successfully play this game called Life.

You'll finally know who's responsible for
getting what you want.

If your life isn't working out the way you want it to,
>*you*
>better make it work your way because
>if you don't
>no one really cares,
>>but *you*.

Everyone else is too busy trying to get their
own act together or
   they're too preoccupied with their own
           private chamber of horrors
           to worry about yours.

When you tell me that
       someone ruined your life or career,
                       it always is a lie.

Did they really screw you?

Did they really "do it to you?"

Whose responsibility is it that your life
became so screwed up?

Whose responsibility is it to see to it
        that it becomes unscrewed?

Giving up the drama –
            Changing the channel –
            Rebooting--
                seems difficult because:

Our minds even function to make us right
about being the Victim and playing
        life from effect.

We have to justify
            and
        make reasonable
        our negative experiences, which brings us to...

STAMP COLLECTIONS

About 60 years ago there was a phenomenon in which people collected trading stamps, called

S & H Green Stamps

The process was simple:

A store would give people a certain number of green stamps based on the amount of their purchase.

The more they bought, the more S&H Green Stamps they were given.

They would then put them into a "Stamp Book", filling it up page by page.

They were also given a "Redemption Center Catalogue" so they could pick out the "free" prize they wanted, such as a lamp, a toaster, or even a "free" holiday trip.

All they had to do was to turn in the appropriate number of books of stamps for the gift.

Finally, people would go to the "Redemption Center" and exchange the books of stamps for their "free" gift.

Dr. Eric Berne noticed that people did the same thing with their experiences from the past. We collect our past feelings and experiences to justify our behavior NOW.

People save "psychological trading stamps" which also come in several colors.

Lots of us love Brown Stamps
(Brown Stamps stand for exactly what you
think Brown Stamps would stand for.)

You collect a Brown Stamp whenever you say
    "Aw shit!"

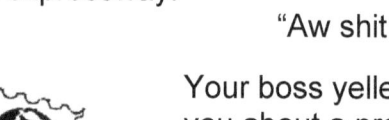

Your alarm clock didn't go off?
    "Aw shit!"

You had a flat tire on the expressway.

                                              "Aw shit!"

                                        Your boss yelled at you about a project you didn't finish on time.

                                        "Aw shit!"

You found the great clothes in a size you *used* to be.
    "Aw shit!"

Eventually…you accumulate enough Brown Stamps to go to the Redemption Center and get a "guilt-free" gift.

With enough Brown Stamps you can have a
        "guilt-free" argument:
            "After all, they deserve it!"
            "Look what they did to me!"

Most arguments are not concerned with
> Here Now –

they're concerned with There Then.

What happens is you take out all of the Brown Stamps that you've ever collected and you both play a wonderful game of
> "Yea, so top that one!"

You can go back years with…

> "You never got up with the kids…"

> "Who had to pay for the car when you crashed it…"

> "You never took me to nice places when we were dating."

You keep going back and forth until you think
> you've won the award for
> "The Smelliest Brown Stamp Collection":

Arguments are often an exchange of bad feelings –
> masquerading for love and caring.

The Brown Stamp Redemption Centre also has "Guilt-Free Quits" from the job.

Have you ever quit a job?

Did you have enough Brown Stamps to justify it?

These would include:

> "I didn't get the raise I deserved."

> "I wasn't invited to the office party!"

" I worked my ass off and that's the thanks I got!"

"My proposal sat on your desk for three months!"

You can also have a "Guilt-Free Divorce."

"After all, who could live with a woman like that?"

"And then he forgot our anniversary again!"

"He never so much as lifted a finger to help with the kids!"

You can have a "Guilt-Free Fire-the-Employee:

"Your performance reviews have been negative"

"If you come to work late one more time…"

"That's the last straw!"

You can even spank your kids, "Guilt-Free:"

    "Now see what you made me do!"

    "I told you three times to stop."

    "How many times do I have to tell you?"

You can even have a "Guilt-Free Suicide" –
   "What's the use in trying."

    "Life is shitty."

    "Nobody loves me."

All in all –the Brown Stamp Redemption Center has some very smelly gifts.

    And yet you're the one saving!

    You're the one with the collection!

No one is forcing you to collect Brown Stamps!

The Truth is you're so ethical that your mind always pays you back —you start to justify, make reasonable and try to be "right" about the most incredibly rotten experiences.

You're not even honest with the Redemption Center!

Let's say you turned in the 82 books of Brown Stamps for the guilt-free quit, for which you had been diligently saving for years.

You walked up to the counter and said:

"Yes, I'd like my guilt-free quit. Here are my 82 books."

That night you didn't know what to do without your collection so...

You drove to the Redemption Center, broke in, and stole all 82 books back! You just didn't know what to do without all that shit!

Notice: If you're saving all that shit, you start to smell.

And a lot of people don't want to be around you.

Of course, you do get to be *Right*.

Someone told you "Life is Shitty" —and you believed it.

However, no one is forcing you to save shit.
    (Or to shovel it for ten years!)
Nobody has a gun to your back saying
    "Save Shit or Else!"

Why don't you just flush your Brown Stamps?

WHOOSH!

Maybe you're like the little toddler who doesn't want Mommy to flush the stuff. You fear that without your Brown Stamps you wouldn't exist.
>(Flush them and find out.)

What good can it possibly do to carry around all that shit?

Get the Joke! "I think I'll save all the shit I can from a past that doesn't exist, so I can justify a shitty experience in the NOW.

Then I'll wonder why my life feels so shitty and why I don't have satisfaction.
>The joke's on you.

Maybe, you should just walk up to someone and say,
>"I'd like to flush something between us."

It's all that stuff that's been keeping you from
>experiencing that person.

Not only do you keep all the negative shit –

But your beliefs that you're not worthy can keep you from experiencing the positive.

If you have a basic belief –"If they really knew me
>they wouldn't like me." —then no one will be able to get close enough to share any of the positive things.

It's all a reflection of you. Your ability to be positive with others is a measure of your own self-esteem.

The positives are called **"Gold Stamps."**

Many are reluctant to accept Gold Stamps when offered. It's as though you say: "Oh, no thanks, I only save Brown."

Someone says: And you say:

"What a great dinner."   "Oh, that's my mom's recipe."

"Good report, Johnson."   "Aw, anyone could do it."

"Congratulations!"   "Just lucky, I guess."

"You did beautifully."   "Aw, it was nothing."

"You look great."   "Really, I've had this rag for years!

There are two magic words that allow you to accept Gold Stamps when offered:

Thank You

Those two words not only allow you to collect Gold Stamps, they also allow you to give them back:

"Thank you, I really enjoy having you over."

"Thank you. How kind of you."

"Thank you for all your assistance."

Not to acknowledge Gold Stamps is to discourage getting them again.

People get tired of acknowledging you, only to have you put down their acknowledgement.
Then you get to be right about no one ever giving you Gold.

You get to be "right" about the color
of stamp you're saving.

Even if I give you a Gold Stamp,
you can paint it any color you wish.

If you're a Brown Stamp collector,
you can paint anything Brown.

If your boss says, "Your report was excellent!"
You can paint it Brown by saying to yourself,

"I bet he says that to everyone."

You can paint it Red for Anger by saying to yourself:

"That S.O.B, if he paid me more, I'd turn in good reports all the time."

Or
You can paint it Blue for Hurt feelings by saying: "Doesn't he (snivel, snivel) think *all* my reports are good?(snivel)"

You can always see what you're looking for.

You create the Drama so you can justify collecting the stamps.

The scenes that take place during the Drama
are called **Psychological Games**:

Psychological Games are behaviors

> -that keep us from acknowledging our responsibility in the matter;
>
> -that allow us to avoid facing that which we are afraid to face;
>
> -that are automatic patterns;
>
> -that keep people distant and from experiencing the true beauty of one another; and
>
> -that keep providing the stamps we like to collect.

Eric Berne named some of the psychological games, in his book, *Games People Play* as follows*:*

WHY DOES THIS ALWAYS HAPPEN TO ME?

LET'S YOU AND HIM FIGHT

DEBTOR

POOR ME

AIN'T IT AWFUL?

YOU GOT ME INTO THIS!

LUSH

HARRIED

UPROAR
LOOK HOW HARD I'VED TRIED!

RAPE-O

NOW SEE WHAT YOU MADE ME DO!

LOOK WHAT YOU'RE DOING TO ME

MARTYR

MINE'S BETTER

WHAT WOULD THEY DO WITHOUT ME?

IF IT WEREN'T FOR YOU!

AND

KICK ME

Psychological Games are very serious and sometimes dangerous.

There are first degree, second degree and third degree games. Just like burns.

A first degree burn is like sunburn; a third degree burn involves skin grafting.

Third degree psychological games usually end in

        The emergency room

        The morgue

        The courtroom

        The prison

        The asylum

        The rehab center

They're real, real risky.
You can easily get your token taken away, maimed, or locked up.

But what is really risky,
      is NOT playing games.
At least when you play *games, as negative as they are, you know how they're all going to turn out.*

But to be on stage, without the script--
      just being there – is risky.

To be authentically <u>yourself</u> is risky.
To play games, to run out your act, is not so risky.

Some people will like your act, some won't.
But at least you can always hide behind your act.
The sad part is that even if other people like your act, they won't even know who YOU are.

SOME PEOPLE MAY NOT LIKE THE WAY YOU ARE

When you're just being who you really are,
    some people will like you
        and some people won't.

The good part is
    those people who like you
        will really like <u>you</u>.

To just be who you are;
    won't create a lot of drama –
    just a lot of satisfaction.

To be someone you're not
    is not only schizophrenic,
    it is very energy-draining.

It's like being
>	on stage
>	>	24/7,
> living the drama
>	>	you're creating
>	>	>	with no curtain call 'till the end.

To be who you really are
>	is to give up
>	>	the drama,
>	>	>	the stamps,
>	>	>	>	the games,
>	>	>	>	>	the act,
>	>	>	>	>	>	to gain your own

>	>	>	>	>	>	>	>	life.

>	Who knows!

>	>	It just may be worth it.

8. BEING THE CAUSE means SATISFACTION – GETTING A LITTLE

The basic difference between those who acknowledge their responsibility
    and those who don't
        is

            those who do, smile more.

They have something called
                Satisfaction.

And isn't that what we're all after?

Our society has lots of notions and beliefs about what will make us happy.

But the basic belief is
> that it
all boils down to

MONEY!

Our society and most of
our institutions
> implicitly or
explicitly
> tell us that money
> will make us
happy.

> But will it?

> What will money buy?

> *Food, clothing, shelter.*

What else?

Transportation, recreation, education, luxuries (toys),phones, laptops, drones, play stations, health services, power, status, entertainment, cosmetic beauty, leisure time…

The list could go on.
> But let's stop here.

The list is long enough
> to expose the greatest belief system
> > that runs our society:

> "MORE IS BETTER"

Wherever you put yourself on the money scale,
> you probably think those people above you have it
> > "wired up right."

So you constantly strive to earn more money.
You say,
> "If I could only get a raise.
> *then*
> I would be happy."

And what that notion does
> is to keep you constantly on the treadmill.

IS MORE REALLY BETTER?

Maybe, just maybe —   More isn't Better.

Maybe, More is just More.

That's all.

And less is just less.
> Not worse.

Is more money really better than less money?

Are rich people happier than poor people?

Are poor people happier than rich people?

(I know, rich people are supposed to be miserable...

I have some bad news:

There are some happy rich people in this world.
It doesn't seem fair,
but that's just the way it is.

But also there are some very happy poor people...
And some very miserable rich people.

Maybe happiness really isn't wired to money.

Money isn't satisfaction; it's just convenience.

Is more food better than less food?
(In order to be a good boy or girl did you really have to finish everything on your plate?)

Does it really make the people in China/ India/Africa/Syria any happier because you're walking around with the extra pounds from the food they may lack?

Are expensive restaurants always better than less expensive restaurants?

You already know the answer to that question.

Is more clothing better than less clothing?

    Many of us have our happiness wired
    to our next suit/dress/coat/pair of shoes/

We have this belief that "it" will make us happy.

And then we get "It."

But once we wear it
               ZAP
No more satisfaction.   Now it's old.

How about luxuries?

How many diamonds, flat screen TV's, mobile phones,
PDA's, computers, motorcycles, campers, swimming pools,
paintings. laptops, homes, wives/husbands, kids,
degrees…
               will it take
               before you become
               happy?

How much plastic surgery is it going to take before you're happy? How many pills will it take?

Is the head of the company more satisfied than the clerk in the accounting department?

Is more entertainment better?

Go to Las Vegas or Hollywood. Notice the overwhelming sense of joy
as the people rush frantically to "take it all in."

How many shows, movies, night clubs, plays, concerts, operas, parties, grand openings will it take to make you happy?

Is more beauty better than less beauty? Is it possible to be beautiful and happy?

(Yes, damn it. And it doesn't seem fair.)

The bad news is some people are rich, beautiful and happy!)

Is it possible to be homely and happy? Of course.

Does more money given to the Church provide a more secure place in heaven?

Is a more expensive church or temple better than a less expensive one?

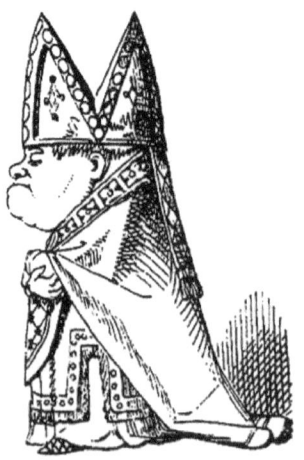

Remember, spirituality is simply that experience of God from within you.

Don't confuse that experience with the institution that creates the
    space for that to occur.

Is more education better than less education?

The belief system is that you have to obtain an advanced degree in order to be happy.

"If only I had a (College Education, a master's degree, or a doctorate…) then I could be happy."

Notice that often the groups with the greatest rate of suicide and divorce are the professionals with advanced education.

Maybe education doesn't make you happy.

There are plenty of miserable people with degrees, and there are plenty of happy people with degrees.

Perhaps education is not better or worse.
        Education is just education.

What about shelter?

Know anyone who feels that if we could just get a larger apartment or home, then we'd be happy?

If we could just
    -buy a vacation house
        -a larger lot
            -add more rooms
                -live in an expensive neighborhood
                        then we'd be happy?

Is more transportation better?

> Are people in chauffeured limousines happier than people in beat-up old Volkswagens?

> Are people who own three cars happier than those people who don't own one?

> Are the first class passengers happier than the coach passengers?

And take a look at how crazy this is.

"More is Better" is literally choking us to death.

Is more recreation better than less? How many times do you need to go

> skiing
> > camping
> > > golfing
> > > > sailing
> > > > > dancing

> > > > > > to make you happy?

Some go often and they're happy.

> Some don't go at all and they're happy.

Is large government better than small government ?

> (Silly question!)

Are more friends better than fewer friends?

Are more "friends" on Facebook or Twitter better than fewer friends?

Is more sex better than less sex?

Ever know anyone getting lots of sex, without any satisfaction
> > > > and vice-versa?

As Eric Hoffer once said: "YOU CAN NEVER GET ENOUGH OF WHAT YOU REALLY DON'T NEED TO MAKE YOU HAPPY."

Going the other extreme doesn't work either.

Less is not better.

Less is just less.

Giving up materialism won't necessarily make you happy,
any more that adding more material objects will make you happy.
The Less-Betters are people who reject money and materialism.

They go around saying, "I just have my jeep and my
      dawg!"

Most Less-Betters often grew up in
      more-better homes.

Mr. And Mrs. More Better had a son, named Les Better.

Les moved out West to "find himself."

He thought that if he gave up everything his parents had, he would be happy.

He felt that materialism and money had robbed them of true happiness.

The sad part was that Les didn't find happiness either.

Materialism – more or less – has little to do with satisfaction.

Money won't make you happy or frustrated. Money is just money.

It is simply convenient to have it. That's all.

It won't make you a better person or
>more satisfied with your experience of life.
>It won't solve your problems for you.

Most of us have been playing "More is Better" for so long, (and there's so much agreement that it's right to play it), that we never bothered to look into our own experience
>to find out if that's
>>where the satisfaction is.

You can't play the game of
>Materialism and have fun,
>as long as your
>"More is Better"
>>belief system stays intact.

However, as soon as
>you're satisfied from within yourself,
>then you can choose
>to play
>MATERIALISM and have a ball.

You'll soon notice that it's all just a game and the purpose of the game is to have fun, not to prove that you're better or more important.

>It's just to have fun.

So it's OK to have more or less –it doesn't matter; just gain some satisfaction in the process.

Some of us have a belief that we can't have satisfaction until we've reached our goal,
>or achieved what we set out to achieve.

Notice what happens with that. We moan and groan
    until we reach our goal.

If we don't reach our goal, we're miserable.

If we do – we're happy… But for how long?

Until the novelty wears off? Until we set our next goal?
Maybe we're just relieved, from the alleviation
                    of the Panic it took to get there.

When we have Satisfaction wired only to achievement or
the end result, we don't get to experience it very often.
It's great to realize that you can be satisfied in the *process*
of attaining your goals.

How often is it possible to experience satisfaction?

Anytime you're willing to
        accept
        what's going on in your experience NOW.

Satisfaction
is a choice
that's made
            NOW.

Satisfaction
    comes from
    experiencing what's
    happening
        Consciously
        and
        Accepting
            the
            Perfection
                of it ALL.

Who determines your satisfaction…?

Who else could? Remember-You're the Cause!

Get the joke when someone tells you that you
         SHOULD be happy?

You either
    are
    or
    you're not.
    (You've stepped into it – or you haven't)

If you wait for happiness to happen to you
        you may wait for a long time.

An ancient Chinese proverb says:

    "Starving man wait long time
    for roast duck to fly into mouth."

You are
    the only one
        who can determine whether you're happy.

No one
    and
        nothing
            can do it for you.

It is your
    fundamental responsibility
        to produce
            satisfaction
                for yourself.

SO HOW DO YOU GET SATISFACTION?

Be Conscious: If you think of times you experienced
>happiness, joy, inner peace and satisfaction,
>were you *there* for it? Of course. In
>order to experience Satisfaction it takes aliveness.

Share the Truth: Satisfaction in a relationship stems from true communication.

To communicate we need to share our experience of self with others
>and be willing to experience the other
>>people
>>the way they are.

You can have relationships of convenience and
>co-existence;
>>but to have love and satisfaction you have to
>>>share the truth.

Satisfaction is present
>to the same degree
>to which you tell the truth
>>in your relationship.

Accept your experience of NOW as Perfect:

According to Webster the definition of Perfect is

"(1)*a state proper to a thing when completed; having all the essential elements characteristics, etc. (2) in a state of complete excellence; faultless, unflawed.*"

To experience satisfaction you simply have to acknowledge the perfection of your experience –
>even with those things you don't like.

Satisfaction is being conscious
    sharing the truth,
    noticing the perfection of your experience,
    accepting total responsibility
    and being the cause.

To be dissatisfied
    is to be playing tapes,

    telling lies,

    withholding the truth,

    assuming no responsibility in the matter

    and being the effect.

Dissatisfaction comes in many unconscious forms:

fear	jealousy
hostility	complaining
anger	blaming
envy	frustration
boredom	embarrassment
tiredness	reasonableness
rightness	hoping
wishing	trying
lying	withholding

Using English, we have a hard time describing Love, Truth, Happiness, and Satisfaction.

But notice the list of unconsciousness could go on forever.

Eskimos have many words for snow —because they live in it.

Likewise, we have no trouble describing negative forms of unconsciousness because we often live in it.

You and only you are the source of your
> satisfaction and dissatisfaction.
>> You have total choice in the matter.

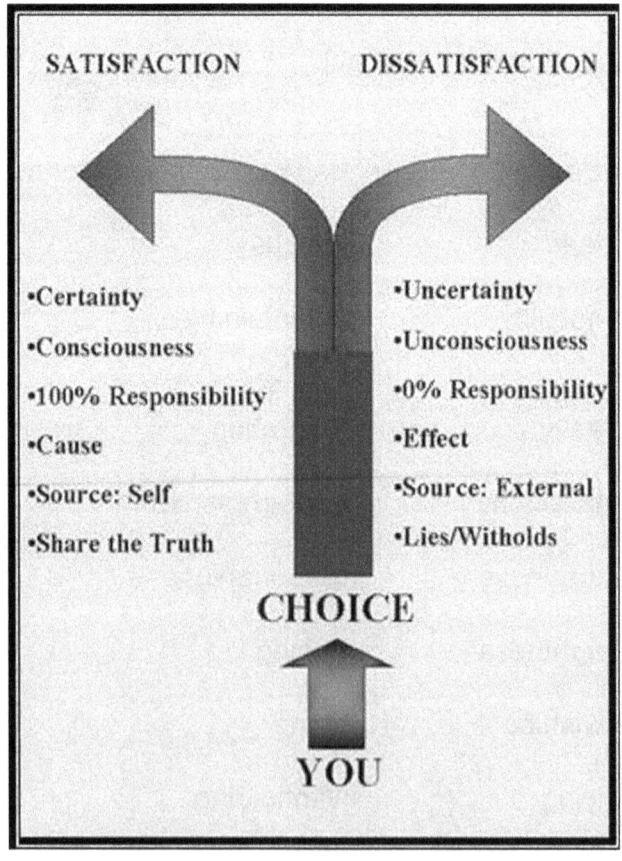

"The Road Not Taken
   Two roads diverged in a wood, and I –
   I took the one less traveled by
   and that has made all the difference."
         -Robert Frost

You are the source of your satisfaction and dissatisfaction.

And you have total choice in the matter.

There's a fork in the road and you get to choose.

The road to satisfaction is an express lane. Very few are dedicated to experience satisfaction in their lives.

The road to dissatisfaction is bumper to bumper. All the agreement is on the side of dissatisfaction.

THE ROAD TO DISSATISFACTION IS BUMPER TO BUMPER

If you're wondering whether you're satisfied-If you have to ask the question, you already have the answer.

How long will it take before you give yourself the permission to be happy?
You can only be satisfied

>Here and Now.

That's all you have.

> Our mind loves to delay our satisfaction
> or to make it a future condition.
>
> "I was happy *when*…"
>
> "I *will* be happy…"
>
> "*If only*… *then* I would be happy…"

NOW is the only space from where we get to play.

Just look at your experience and tell the truth about it.

Telling the truth about yourself produces satisfaction and direction.

Satisfaction is

> where you want it,
>
> when you want it,
>
> how you want it.
>
> Just let it be and be there with it,
>
> And get a little!

9. BEING THE CAUSE means MAKING AND KEEPING COMMITMENTS

Once we know what we want, then all we have to do is set up the process to get it.

The process has to do with formulating and keeping commitments.

An agreement is a mutual commitment to produce a result.

If you want to produce a result with someone,
first, you'll have to agree upon the result that you want to accomplish.

> Then, you'll have to tell the truth about it.
> And finally, you'll have to do what's necessary to get it.

Once you're aware of how the universe is set up,

it's like directing a very well-rehearsed orchestra—

when it's time for the violins to come in…………the violins come in.

In order for your life to work, it must be based on commitments.

    Your relationships,
        your job,
           your company,
              your marriage,
                  all produce satisfaction to the
                  extent that you make and keep
                  your commitments.

Not to keep a commitment is to become the effect of the relationship. You get to be right and dissatisfied.

A neurotic is a person who continually makes commitments with himself and then breaks them.

Neurotic behavior is to make commitments with others
    with no intention of keeping them.

You pay yourself back for not keeping your commitments.

    You can make a lot of money and not keep commitments.
        You can have lots of possessions, be famous, be respected and not keep commitments.

    You can have it all and have nothing.

    The bottom line of satisfaction is
        you either have it or you don't.

How long are you going to continue to lie to yourself?

If you don't have satisfaction
    in your relationship,
    on your job,
    or with your friends…
        There's a lie.

Look for a commitment that has not been fulfilled.

Remember that people don't break agreements *on* you,
    only *with* you.

The truth is *you* are.

    If you notice a lot of dissatisfaction and broken agreements with others –rather than blaming *them*, you'd better ask yourself, what you're getting out
        of the situation.

Why do you have people in your experience who don't keep their commitments with you?

Maybe you don't need to play the Victim of broken agreements.
If you have broken agreements look for the underlying truth.

In order for an agreement to work, it has to be perceived as being mutually beneficial, otherwise, no result is produced.

A relationship that only serves one person doesn't last.

Remember that the stake we're playing for
    is not the result itself.

The stake we're playing for
    is the sense of satisfaction.

And that makes it alright to go ahead and play
    to produce results.

The basis of an agreement is the
    truth.

If you don't tell the truth, take a look at
    who gets damaged.

If you really want to do damage to yourself,
    blame the other person for not producing the result.

    Go ahead and lie about your responsibility in the matter.

Look at the illusion that a partnership is a 50-50 proposition.
There you sit saying, "Well, I did my 50%, where's his?"

Playing it from 50-50 just doesn't work.

The problem is that if your partner falls down, you have to pay the bill. There's no 50-50 in the universe... not from where *you* sit.

You'll get 100% of whatever you're willing to take responsibility for getting.

If you enter into an agreement and your partner lies, what you'll notice is that you set it up for your partner to lie.

Then you lied to yourself when you refused to look at it.

The only thing that can't lie is the result.

All you have to do is look at the result you said you were committed to producing, and that'll tell you if one or both of you have been lying.

When you let a broken agreement slide,
    through hoping and wishing,
        you may begin to notice that you've been
            withholding and lying,
                and you just gave up your satisfaction.

Playing from the truth
    doesn't seem as easy
        until you do it.

Then it will become obvious that there's no other way to play.

It isn't that it's wrong to lie. It just doesn't work.

Every time you tell a lie, it'll rob you of your satisfaction.

If you enter into an agreement that you're unwilling to keep, it'll be like a boomerang thrown into the universe.

    It'll hit you on the head every time.

        Let's look at an example:

I ask Mary to have lunch with me on Monday at noon in the new Italian restaurant. Because it's close to where she works, she agrees to meet me there.

We have an agreement to produce a mutually beneficial result.

        On Monday I show up at 12:00 and guess what?

                No Mary!

My typical response would be to

blame,
moan,
groan,
worry,
reach for my Brown Stamp book
and make Mary wrong.

(Notice that to blame others is to create a new automatic response or to reinforce old *ones*.)

How much responsibility do I take for Mary not showing?

    -0-Zero-None-Zilch-

    ("Well, I was there on time! I kept my part
    of the agreement!   I put in my 50%!")

What's the truth?

I am totally responsible for my reaction
to the event. I am also responsible for the event itself. I didn't do everything
    necessary to produce the result.

She didn't do it to me.   I did it to me.

I did everything necessary for the situation to be exactly the way it was.

Am I at fault or am I to blame?
No, I am just the cause.

Fault and blame are really asking whether you are wrong.

Being the cause is neither being right or wrong.

To find fault or to identify blame is just an evaluation of the event. And if you think about it, evaluations are useless chatter.

Often after the event passes,
    after a week, month, or year,
        we'll notice the perfection of an event
            that we originally judged to be
                awful, frightening, or terrible.

To be "cause" is to notice the perfection at the instant of its occurrence.

The experience of Mary not showing up is perfect.

It's just hard to realize that when you're playing from effect. To determine that you are cause, ask,
    "Did I do *everything* necessary to produce the result?"

Results don't lie.

    I didn't call to see if she had seen the SMS or email to remind her.

    I didn't pick her up.

    I didn't tell her lunch was "on me."

I didn't tell her exactly where I would meet her.
    I didn't tell her how important lunch was for me.

        I didn't make sure she was conscious when I made the agreement.

When things like that happen to you, you should ask yourself, "What do I get out of having it be this way?"

Maybe you get to make Mary wrong, because she made you wrong once. (Retaliation) or

    you get to feel sorry for yourself, "Why does this
        always happen to me?"
                or

        you get to manifest your biased belief systems:
        "Just like a woman to forget about lunch!"

There are all sorts of reasons you'd do that to you,
        and you're the only one who knows the truth.

And do you want to know the real kick in the kimono?

You both knew when you made the agreement
that it wouldn't work.

Somehow I knew she would stand me up and so did she. You know when you making an agreement whether it's the truth
                or
                not,
                or
                whether you're both lying.

It makes total nonsense out of playing the game.

You typically know at the time that you have no intention of keeping the agreement.
You know that the agreement is unreasonable or just
        wishful thinking. Or something just tells you,
            "It'll never work."

When you think of times—

> when you kept your agreement –
>
> when you produced the result –
>
> when you did it –

didn't you know you'd do it when you made the agreement?

And when you didn't keep the agreement...

> didn't you know that would happen when you made the agreement
>
> > in the first place?

When did you know the marriage wouldn't work?
("Oh, before we got married.")

When did you know that this wasn't the right job for you? ("Oh, before I was hired.")

When did you know that you wouldn't finish the task? ("Oh, when I told myself I would.")
What a joke!

At work your supervisor asks if you can produce a thousand widgets and you say, "Sure."
> (And the voice inside your head is going nuts:
> "You'll never be able to do that!"
> "A thousand widgets? That's crazy!")

That's called
Management by Wishes.
"I sure *wish* I could, boss."

"I sure *wish* you could too."

And then you spend the rest of the time trying, effort-ing,
>   coming up with excuses, justifications,
>   reasonableness, and
>   rightness!

Life is Results or Bullshit.

You are either producing the results on time, as agreed, or
you're producing the bullshit
as to why you haven't produced the results.

Bullshit comes packaged in many forms:
>   reasonableness,
>   belief systems,
>   excuses,
>   justifications,
>   being right,
>   blaming other people
>   circumstances,
>   or events.

The instant you
comprehend that you've lied about the agreement, you
immediately start to blame and assign cause elsewhere.
>   It's not a very fun game.

Results lead to satisfaction, completeness, and fulfillment.

Bullshit leads to more bullshit.

And it's all Unc-ing out.

It's all Theatre of the Absurd

when you realize that companies spend more time and energy producing Bullshit rather than the results they said they wanted.

And everyone knew that it was all going to turn into Bullshit at the beginning of the process.

It's as though everyone said ,"Let's create Bullshit,
lie about it, go Unconscious together and get paid in the
process."

It's totally amazing that some companies survive.
Bullshit takes hours, and hours, and more hours.

If you can't come up with enough justifications
and excuses yourself, you can formulate a committee to
help you.

A committee is a B.S. producing machine.

If you're producing results, there's not much to talk about
except to say: "We did it!"

If you're not producing results, "OMG, the excuses, the
rightness, the justifications, the reasonableness, you can
come up with…"

It takes hours, and becomes very dramatic, since it's all
from the Effect state.

Sales people who are producing results don't have time for
meetings and conferences with their managers.

Those who aren't producing results,
    need a lot of management time to complain about
        bad leads,
        flaky customers,
        the bad time of year,
        the bad economy,
        poor training,
        bad sales tools
        too few ads, etc., etc., etc.
According to Lao Tzu in 600 B.C.,

    "Those who know, don't talk.
    Those who talk, don't know."

You accept responsibility when you're producing results and keeping your commitments.

> "Did you do everything necessary to produce the result?"
> Of course, or you wouldn't have the result.

And when you are not producing the results and not keeping your agreements, you scream "I'm not responsible!"

Your mind resists the 100% responsibility clause. It doesn't like it.

However, this is not a ploy to convince you;
> it's just a report on how the universe works.

Every time you made an agreement and it worked, both parties took 100% responsibility, (i.e., did everything necessary to produce the result) to make it work.

How long are you going to lie about having no responsibility when the agreement doesn't work?

Every time you lie, you produce more bullshit for you to shovel.

You produce so much yourself, you don't need any help from the "four-legged" varieties.

A manager from a large life insurance agency just didn't want to acknowledge his 100% responsibility.

He said that if he had ten agents, who made an agreement to each have a million dollar sales year, then he would make an agreement with his boss for ten million dollars in volume for his office.

He really had trouble seeing how **he** was responsible if **they** broke their agreements.

Consider the reverse:

If they did keep their agreements, would he take responsibility for them producing the results? You bet cha!

He would have done everything necessary to insure that the results were produced.

He would have worked with the agents who were having problems, provided special incentives, held weekly meetings and progress reviews, presented special sales seminars, insured good, qualified leads, etc. He would have well-deserved the pat on his back from his boss.

What about when the result wasn't produced? It was _their_ fault!

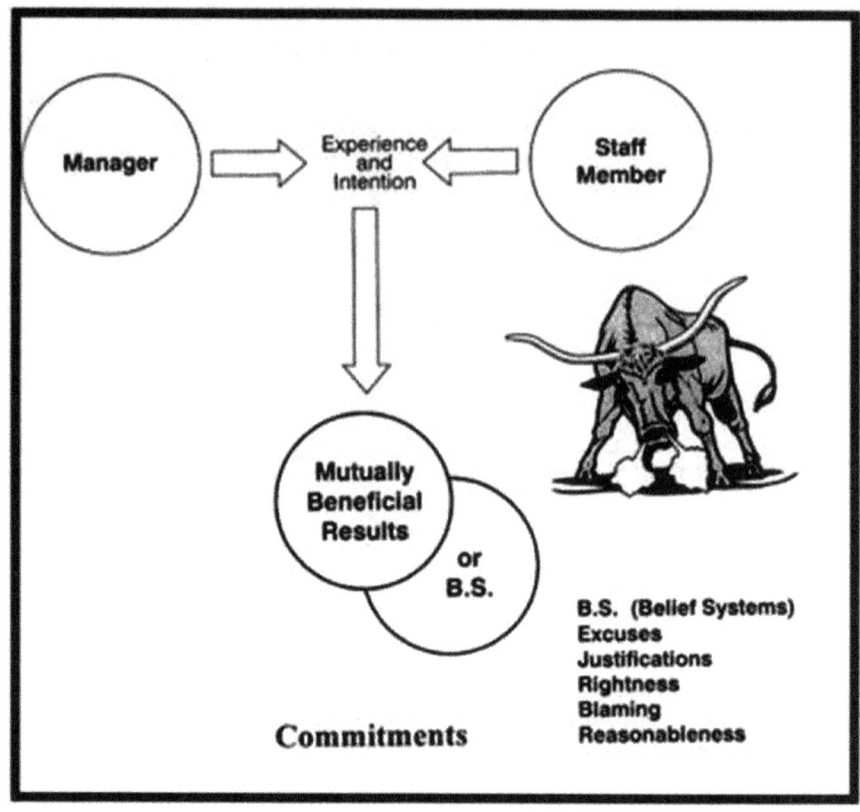

(Keep shoveling!)

The truth would be that he did absolutely everything necessary <u>not</u> to produce the result.

He didn't work with the agents who were having problems, or provide special incentives, etc., etc., etc.

You are totally responsible for everything in your experience.

Your intention is your experience.
Your experience is your intention.

Yeah, but...how can I be responsible...

    for the computer crashing?

    for the financial melt-down?

    for the building burning?

    for my manager quitting?

    for the contractor going on strike?

Remember, the question isn't "How?"-- unless you're big on
    Bio-gravitational,
    self-organizing field forces,
    the law of attraction and quantum physics.

The question is "What?"

"What am I getting out of having it be this way?"

"What can I learn from this experience?"

Complaining about it doesn't change the negative.

It only makes it reasonable to yourself and others.

In order for life to work smoothly, it takes you doing what's necessary to keep your commitments with yourself and others and promoting relationships with others that are mutually beneficial.

10. BEING THE CAUSE means GETTING WHAT YOU WANT AND WANTING WHAT YOU GET

People play games to see if they can win. Some of us play life the same way.

The only thing wrong with that is that you think you have to win to experience satisfaction.

What about the rest of the time you're playing life?

Life is like a chart that goes up and down. It has peaks and valleys. That's the drama we create with a series of Now's.

Playing to win is drawing an arbitrary line and saying, "I'll be
happy at that point."

Notice that a "win" only lasts one instant of Now. So if you're playing to win, you're using up all your time to get one instant of satisfaction.

>"Wins" may not come too often.

So how can you change it to make more sense? The first step is to set a goal.

Goals produce results. Results produce satisfaction.

You can't get that which you don't know you want.

What you want could be out there in the universe and you wouldn't recognize it.

If you are unclear about your goals, you don't have any.

What you have are wishes not goals.

To accomplish your goals you must have clarity. As long as you think your wishes are you goals you won't be able to reach them.

THERE'S A DIFFERENCE BETWEEN
A GOAL AND A WISH!

In order to get what you want, get

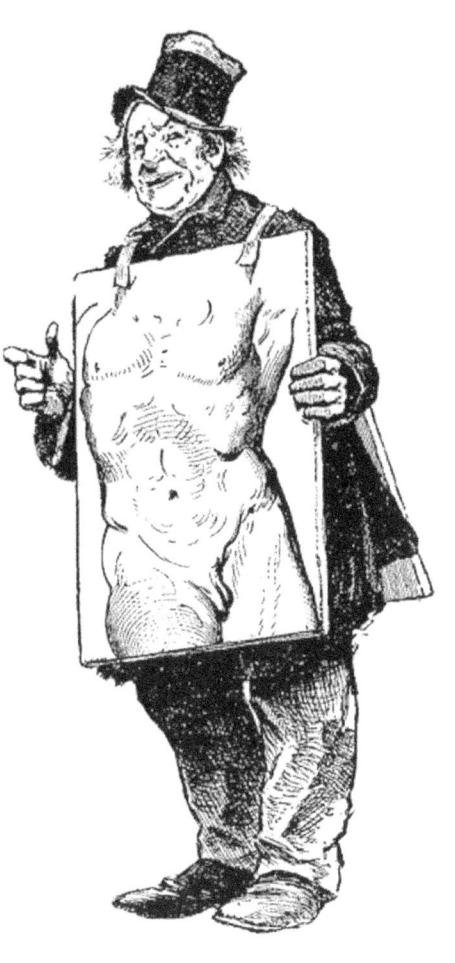

<u>S</u>

<u>M</u>

<u>A</u>

<u>R</u>

<u>T</u>

about your goals.

For a goal to be a goal, and not a wish, it must be:

Specific:

Until a goal is specific, it doesn't require concrete action.
"I'd like to lose some weight," doesn't
get the job done.
"I want to increase productivity," is
a wish.
Getting specific avoids future complaining.

If I tell my secretary to buy a new chair for the office, she could buy a rocking chair or a typing chair, and then I could roar,
"I didn't want *that* kind of chair!"

Wishes have no reality, no substance.

If you want to get what you want, be as specific as possible.

BE SPECIFIC!

*M*easurable:

To determine whether you've accomplished your goal, it must be measurable.

Making it measurable lets you know whether you've accomplished it. Notice the difference between
        "I'd like to lose some weight," and
        "I'm going to lose three pounds this month."

*A*cceptable:

To be acceptable, both the goal and the means to accomplish the result must be ethical.

"I'm going to lose three pounds next month by taking diuretics and speed," is not acceptable.

"I'm going to have 10,000.00 bucks in the bank next year," is a fine goal unless you plan to embezzle the money.

We are totally ethical beings. Responsibility brings together all of your moral and ethical considerations. The end does not justify the means.

Lying,
    cheating
        and stealing
            just don't work.

  They won't produce what we want the goal to
        produce
          —what we're after –
              satisfaction.

    You may find that you are unwilling to do what's necessary to produce the result, if the result or the means are unethical.... (and you always know).

_R_*ealistic:*

If you have unrealistic goals, who are you kidding? Look what happens: "I want to lose fifteen pounds next month," and then you only lose five. All that does is allow you to feel badly that you didn't accomplish your goal.

People who set realistic goals for themselves, and then accomplish those goals, feel good about themselves. People who set their goals too low, feel badly, because "Anybody could have done it."

Some have it wired that they win when they lose, and others have wired that they lose when they win. Why not win when you win?

_T_*ruthful:*

Is the goal the Truth? You are the only one who knows for certain. If the goal isn't the truth, it will get stuck in your tube and once again, you'll suffer from cosmic constipation.

The process of becoming
  S pecific,
  M easurable,
  A cceptable,
  R ealistic,
  T ruthful
        is taking responsibility for the goal.

And that is SMART.

There's just no way to take responsibility for what is beneficial until you know what you want.

Satisfaction comes from telling the truth about what you want and doing what's necessary to get it.

ABILITY

The second thing you have to do to get what you want is to determine whether you have the *ability* to accomplish the goal you've set for yourself.

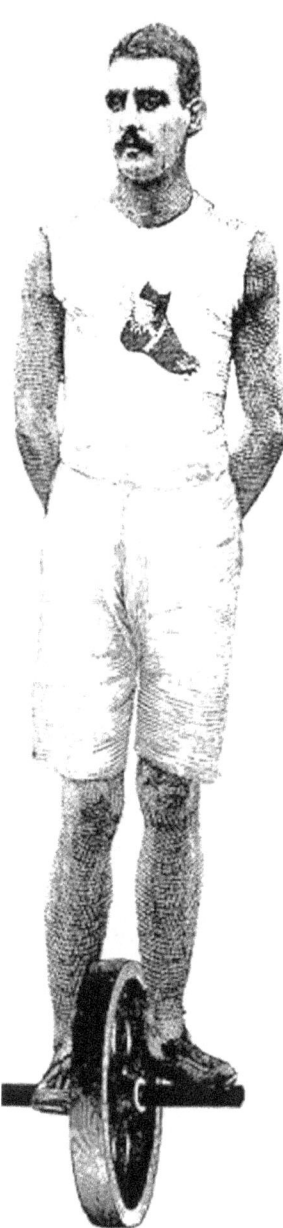

You either have it, or you don't.

That's all there is to say about your ability.

How do you know whether you have the ability?

You know it like you know the Truth.

Perhaps you like to play from "Poor little me, I just don't have the ability."

Notice how effectively that helps you
        avoid responsibility.

We were all born with incredible ability; we've just managed to cover it with a phenomenal amount
        of B.S.

"I don't think I have the ability." is a taped response that keeps you from finding out whether you do or you don't.

It allows you to play from
        5%-20%-40%-60%-80%-90%
The fear is that if you put 100% of *you* out there, it may not be enough!

And if you fail you might get embarrassed!

You might not get everyone's approval.
Don't worry about it.

>You have an incredible amount of ability.
>You have all the ability you need.

Every time you're willing, you'll find the ability necessary to accomplish the result. That is, unless you're addicted to B.S.

The B.S. makes a wish out of a goal.
You create a wish when you say you have a goal and
>you don't have the ability to accomplish it.

Let's say that your goal is to run
>a twenty-five mile marathon and win.

That sounds like a good goal until you state that you're in a wheelchair.
>"Poof!"
>The goal just became a wish.

A lot of people play life wishing from wheelchairs.

So, if you're
>SMART
about your goals and
>if you have the
>>ability —
>>>all you have to do is
>>>>Do it!

To accomplish a goal —
>to get what you want —
>>you have to take RESPONSIBILITY.

Who's responsible for the achievement of a goal?
>The myth is that it depends on other people.
>(And we know what that's all about!)

The only scarce commodity in the universe is people willing to take total responsibility.

The test to determine whether you're willing to take responsibility is to ask yourself:

"Am I willing to do what's necessary to accomplish the goal?" The answer is "Yes" or "No."

Not "Almost." Not "Maybe." Not "To a certain extent." Not "If it is convenient."

The only way to get what you want
          is
    for you to do <u>everything</u> necessary to
        get it.
It only can work that way.
      The rest of the B.S. is not only ridiculous,
        but utter nonsense.

You've probably been waiting for Good Luck
                for a long time.

    It just hasn't seemed to have materialized.

Funny,
    the instant you take responsibility
    for what you want,
    somehow you get "lucky" as hell!!
    You become tremendously "Fortunate."

According to Campbell, "People who want milk should not seat themselves on a stool in the middle of a field in hopes that a cow will back up to them."

You have to do everything necessary.

                                          Everything.

When you first state a goal, you say,
> "I want that."

In order to get it, you have to start on the path of doing everything that's required to get it.

What happens if you stop half-way?
> You won't get it.

> No matter what else is going on.

> If you stop at 99%-- it's no result.

                          Everything means *everything*.

For example, I'm a lousy skier.

I ski by tumbling down mountain sides.

I could tell myself that I have a goal of becoming an expert skier in two years.

> Do I have the ability? The answer is clearly "yes."

> Am I willing to do everything necessary in order to accomplish the goal?

> The answer is "no."

> I'm not willing to take ski instructions, to go out on the slopes every weekend, to buy good equipment, to stand in the long lines, etc.

Therefore, my goal just became a wish:

> "I sure *wish* I could become an expert skier."

Every time you set something as a goal and it's really a wish,
        it gets stuck in your tube.

It's much easier to tell the truth about it at the beginning of the process than to get it stuck.

Why even start the process?

Don't start things that you're unwilling to take responsibility for completing.

Why not set up the universe up to serve you?

When you tell the truth about what you want,
        you literally create it.

        You don't get stuck in it.

When you complain about what's going on or say that someone or something else is responsible,
        life gets real heavy.

If what you're doing doesn't work, you have to ask,

        "What's the source of the problem?"

        "What are all the belief systems (B.S.) between me and having it be
            the way I say I'd like it to be?"

        "Woulda"
            "Coulda"
                "Shoulda"
                    are all ridiculous statements.

The idea that you could have done something
        that you didn't,
            is psychotic.

Perhaps you have a belief system
                that you have to "effort"
                              at accomplishing a goal.

TRYING IS NOT DOING

"Trying" is usually an excuse for not doing. It is a concept employed to justify self-defeat.

Have you ever "tried" to get to sleep at night?
    The harder you try, the more awake you become.
Have you ever "tried" to lose weight?
    All you're saying is you're effort-ing at what you're not doing.
Have you ever "tried" to quit smoking, drinking, medicating, snorting, shooting up…?
    "Trying to quit" means you're still doing it,
                and effort-ing like hell not to.
In the real world there are no "A's" for effort,
        only for producing results.

If you think you're working your ass off, turn around and
        check to see if it's still there.

Perhaps you have a belief system that says,
    "I never have enough time…"

This is an inaccurate statement.

>   You have all the time there is.
>   No one in the universe
>   has more time than you do.

You never *have* time.   You *create* time.

>   You choose to do what's necessary during that period.

Maybe you like to run the mental tape, "I just can't afford it."

There's no scarcity of money in the universe.

There's more money than you could possibly spend.

>   "Can't" typically translates into "Won't."

When you say "I can't"
 you're putting the responsibility outside of yourself.

"I won't…" assumes cause, responsibility and choice.

"I can't afford it," means, "I won't do whatever is necessary to be able to afford it."

"I just *CAN'T* talk to
                    my boss,
                    my spouse,
                    my kid,
                    my parents,
equates to
"I WON'T do what's necessary to
                    communicate effectively."

And many times it means "I won't get off my position of right-ness."

Stop lying to yourself and to those other people who need to hear the truth from you.

If you want help in formulating your "Can'ts" you can create a committee, an agency, an organization or even family members to help you.

Groups of like-minded "Can't" people can continually reinforce each other's beliefs.

When individuals aren't responsible enough to stand up for what they believe,
  they can hope for a group decision,
    absolving them individually,
      since "they" made the decision,
        or "we" thought it best..

That's why the phrase, "Yes, we CAN," is so inspiring for some and so threatening for others at the same time.

There's a realization that it's total nonsense to persist in an activity that doesn't produce results.
You need to ask yourself:
"How many times have I done things that
haven't been true to my purpose?"

It takes a lot of careful, unconscious planning to screw it up and feel justified about it. The truth is you get what you unconsciously intended to get or get what you got because you were unconscious.

Not to get what you said you wanted is to have lied about your prior intention.

To become conscious about your intentions is to make happen what's happening-- directionally.

To get what you truly intend to get...

        Clarify your goals.

        Be SMART about them,

        Check to see if you have the ability,

and then take responsibility for making it happen. That's when your life starts to expand because responsibility involves the awareness, that you choose every moment of
        NOW.

Coming from a position of choice and being the cause allows you the freedom to be who you are –
and who you are to become.

"IF YOU DON'T KNOW WHERE YOU'RE GOING, YOU CAN'T GET THERE, AND YOU CAN'T GET ANYWHERE UNTIL YOU KNOW WHO YOU ARE."
        -SENECA

11. BEING THE CAUSE means MAKING YOUR RELATIONSHIPS WORK

A Relationship is a series of agreements to produce results.

The best relationships produce Satisfaction.

In any Relationship, it's important to ask:

> What do I want out of this Relationship?

> What am I willing to put into it?

For the Relationship to last, the answer to those questions needs to balance.

Expect too much, without giving, and you'll go unconscious with
> Blame, Disappointment and Frustration.

Give more than you're getting, and you'll go unconscious with
> Resentment, Wishes and Hopes.

If you're not getting enough from your relationships –

at work,
　with your boyfriend or girlfriend,
　　with your spouse,
　　　with your children,
　　　　with your friends –
then you're probably playing from Effect State:

> They're doing it _to_ you, or not doing it _for_ you.

> And you keep waiting for it all to happen to you.

To be the Effect of your Relationship
　is to produce B.S. rather than Satisfaction.

Of course, the B.S. does give you something to talk about over coffee, at cocktail parties, at the beauty salon, the gym, on the phone, or on the golf course…

> If your relationships are working, there's not much to say.
> 　(If your shoes fit, you don't feel them.)

All you have to do to get the relationship to work is
　to take responsibility
　　for what's happening.

Just take responsibility for what's going on already,
    in the Here and Now,
        and you've won.

        It's very simple.

If you assume a
        Causal Position
    rather than an
        Effect State

    in your relationships,

you may be able to experience satisfaction
throughout the relationship
        in   both
        the   ups
and
        the   downs.

Relationships are two sided – you and me.

When you enter into a relationship, you must accept it as 100%-100%,
    not 50%-50%.

You have to take responsibility for the other person. As well as yourself. To say, "Well, that's <u>their</u> problem" is a nasty little joke.

Look again.
You may not like it that way.
    That's just the way it is.

If you enter into a relationship and say, "I have no control over my partner," that's a lie.

And you know it's a lie because when the bill comes due,
    guess who pays it!

If your partner doesn't do what *you* want, it's your experience that suffers.

So if you want your relationship to serve you,

    you must be willing to reach out
    and take the 100% responsibility you have
    in order to make it work.

Once you realize that you created the situation

    exactly the way it is right now,

        you'll also notice that the

    person with whom you have the relationship
    is exactly
    the type of person you asked
        Central Casting
        to send over.

The person doesn't have to change in order to be who they are.

Take a look at how much energy
>   we put into getting the other
>   person to change –
>   (Not too effective, is it?

You'll always be miserable
>   as long as you're complaining about your relationship
>   or blaming the other person
>   for what you're experiencing.

Too often we demand that the other person change and then gripe when they don't.

As Werner Erhard once said:
>   "IT'S EASIER TO RIDE THE HORSE IN THE DIRECTION IT'S GOING!"

Waiting for the other person to change allows you to be right.

Being right may destroy the relationship.

You always lose.

Even if you win, you lose, because you get to play alone…
>   And that's why you entered the relationship
>   in the first place –
>   so you wouldn't have to play alone.

"Right" and "Wrong" are really two sides of the same coin.

It doesn't make any difference who's right and who's wrong.

If the result of being satisfied is not produced, you're both lying. And there's no right or wrong in that.

Who says what's right and what's wrong,
        and does any of it matter if you're not satisfied?

In your original agreement, you said, "I want to…
        work with –
           -love-
              -be with you."

Not "I want to be right when I'm with you."

If you and I are fighting and both of us are unwilling to stop fighting,
        nothing will happen.
    Neither of us is willing to move from our
        position of rightness.

To get relationships to work, you have to be willing to play from a position other than Right/Wrong.

Take a look at what might happen if you just unilaterally –
        (without asking anybody *for* anything;)
        (without asking your partner to *do* anything;)
      communicated the truth about what was going on.

All you'd have to do is give up your position about being right.

Not being Right will allow you to experience your
 relationship from a Causal position.

Being the Cause of what's happening in your relationship
is to acknowledge

 that you had total choice all along;
 that you are getting something out of having the
  relationship be the way it is;
 that you have choice right now

  to continue the relationship as is,
   or
  to change within the relationship,
   or
  to end the relationship.

If Love and Satisfaction are what you're after,
 you may have to confront certain beliefs and myths:
  i.e., that you're not worthy of love.
   that happiness really isn't possible,
   that this relationship is "alright" until
    the "real" one comes along.

The Truth is
    you are worthy of all the love anyone can muster
    and you're worthy of satisfaction in all of
    your relationships.
    Why would you set it up any differently?
    Why have you?
You have choices.
All you have to do is to look and see whether the relationship you have right now serves you or not.

If the relationship serves you, keep it and enjoy it.
If it doesn't serve you
    either take responsibility for changing it,
    accept it and make the best of it, or
    get out of the relationship.
    (Now that's dog doo simple!)
    You don't need to be a martyr.

A lot of us love to play from,

"I'm in this relationship and I don't like it the way it is."

Complaining about it is ridiculous.

If you don't like the relationship, *choose* to do something about it.

The height of nonsense is to stay in a relationship that doesn't serve you and gripe about it!

What good does it do you to complain to someone else because you relationship isn't working?

Does it serve you to moan and groan about your boss to your spouse?

Or to gripe about your spouse to a friend?

When you complain, your relationship stays the same.

    You just get to go Unc for a while.

If your relationship isn't working, you're the one suffering.

The only virtual reality you can play is called, "My Experience."
That's all you have.

There's nothing else in the game for any of us.

If you're in a relationship that doesn't serve you, look at the lie.

You may have to take responsibility by re-negotiating basic agreements…
    this time based on the truth.

If your relationship isn't working,
                                one or both of you lied.
If you told the truth and the other person lied –
        (which is usually the way *you* see it) –
                and
    you allowed the situation to persist,
        that too becomes a lie.
           You're in it
                    just
                          as
                                deep
                           .

If I can't say I lied
        until you say you lied,
            neither of us
                will ever tell the truth.

If re-negotiating the agreements doesn't work, to clean up the relationship, you may have to dissolve it.

If the other party is unwilling to tell the truth, it doesn't serve you to maintain the relationship.

Some people are willing to live with the lies.

They really *expect* others
to lie to them.

They persist in relationships based on lies, and then indulge in blame.

The most important commitment to make in any relationship is a willingness to share the truth whenever it becomes apparent.

With Truth comes Love.

Admit the Truth about your relationship.

> If it serves you and you have satisfaction –
> keep it the way it is.

> If it doesn't –take some action.

If you don't take action, nothing will happen.

Everybody will keep waiting for it to work out for them.

> How long are you going to wait?

If you don't like the relationship the way it is,
> choose to do something about it,
> because
> you'll continue to be miserable
> as long as you continue to moan about it.

Keeping your agreements allows you to put your headphones on and listen to the symphony of life.

ON MARRIAGE

Marriage involves the
transformation
of *me* into
the *we* of us.

A good marriage
means creating an environment where your partner can be
authentically real,
   without fear
      of repercussions

      of negation

      of retaliation

      of judgment:

-A Free Space-

based on love and respect and ultimate kindness.

No games.
> No negative stamps.
>> No Right/Wrong.
>>> No tally sheets.

Unfortunately, many of us have strange notions about marriage.

Since many of us felt incomplete and unworthy as youngsters, so we were compelled to find someone
> to make us feel whole;
>> to make us feel worthy,
>>> to make us feel loved.

Marriage was a means to work out a solution to a problem.
> The problem was:
>> "I'm alone."

Many of us chose to play a great fantasy.

Some women play from "Some day my Prince will come... He'll sweep me off my feet and we'll live happily ever after."

Some men play from "Some day I'll find my damsel-in-distress... I'll slay the Dragon, and I'll take my Beautiful Princess away and we'll live happily ever after."

That makes for great "Fairy Tale" material. It just doesn't seem to work that way in "The Real World."

The problem with that is, after the honeymoon is over...
　　…or after three years
　　　　…or after seven years
　　　　　　…or after twenty years,

You might wake up one morning,
　　roll over,
　　　　catch a glimpse of your spouse,
　　　　　recoil,
　　　　　　and say,

"God… That's no Prince or Princess! I've been tricked! That's a human being!"

It's at exactly that point that most people start giving less to the relationship and start saving some energy and feelings for the "real" Prince or Princess when they come along.

At first, it's,

> "I'll just give 90% to this marriage
> 　　and
> save 10% for the real Prince or Princess."

Then it's "I'll just give 75% to this marriage and save 25%…"

Of course, eventually it's, "Hell, why should I give more than 40% to this relationship?

> After all I'm looking for the real Prince or Princess to give the other 60%."

Before you know it,

    you're only giving 10% to the marriage

        and wondering
    why it's not working.

Everyone keeps waiting for the game to work out.

They keep waiting for the game to be won...

without noticing that the game is already won, when you become "one."

WAITING FOR IT ALL TO HAPPEN

It was won the instant you said,

"I love you."

That's all you had to say and that's all there is to say.

Marriage only becomes a chore
    when you'd rather be with
        someone-other-than-who-you're-with.

That's when the Drama starts, when the curtain opens...

Ever notice when someone's marriage isn't working, they'll start sharing the Drama about how they are the "effect" of the relationship and their spouse "is doing it to them"?

It's easy to play Victim in marriage, because there's so much drama to be had.

If you play the Victim,
> you'll need a spouse to be a
>> Persecutor or Rescuer.

People enter the union, unconsciously, seeking
> the other player to make the Drama complete.

If the female plays Rescuer,
> and her husband is the Victim,
>> it's called a "Mommy-Atta Boy" relationship.

Mommies take care of their Atta Boys.

They buy their clothes,

make their lunches,

pat them on their behinds

and tell them
> to be a "good-boy" at work.

Atta Boys spend their whole lives being good and nice so Mommy will say,

> "Atta Boy, you did just fine!"

If the male plays Rescuer and his wife takes on the Victim role, its' a "Big Daddy-Snookims" relationship.

Big Daddy loves to rescue his little Snookims.

She's his little "baby-doll."

And he proves it to the rest of the boys
by buying her furs, diamonds and fancy cars.

Like Atta Boy, Snookims runs to Big Daddy to
solve her problems for her –

>(she, being more than just a little on the helpless side)

>And he more than willingly rescues her.

If the male plays Persecutor and his wife is the Victim it's a "Bastard-Poor Dear" relationship.

He's the Bastard,
always
making her
cower to his
whims and
desires…
(The Poor
Dear)

She cooks,
cleans, runs
errands,
and slaves for
him,
while he
shows no
appreciation.

After all, she's
simply fulfilling
her "wifely"
duties.

(The Poor Dear.)

In social settings, the Poor Dear looks haggard, plain, and pained.

The Bastard is often
domineering,
    boisterous,
        obnoxious,
            talking about how he spends money--
                      usually on himself.

                    (The Bastard)

The reverse is where the female is Persecutor
and her husband is the Victim:
the "Bitch-Nice Guy" relationship.

The Bitch rules the roost.

The Nice Guy spends his life, working like a dog,
to make her happy, which is a never-ending task.

All of the Nice Guy's friends feel sorry for him
and constantly ask themselves,
"How did a Nice Guy like Charlie get messed up
with a Bitch like that?"

One of the Nice Guy's favorite pastimes is to escape
the tirades of the Bitch,
go to the local bar,
and relate the latest Drama:

"You shoulda seen what she did to me this time!"

This is how it all looks on the Drama Triangle:

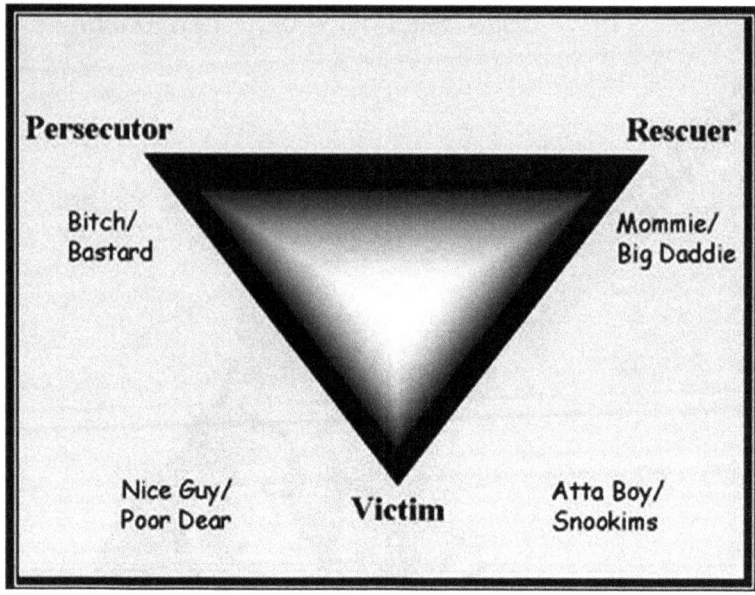

Go to any cocktail party, any bar, any coffee house or any restaurant –and listen to the Drama.

The sad part is the lie.
The lie is "I have no choice in the matter."
The truth is each player has total choice and is the cause in the matter.

Bastards choose Poor Dears and Poor Dears choose Bastards. Bitches choose Nice Guys and Nice Guys choose Bitches. Mommies choose Atta Boys and Atta Boys choose Mommies. Daddies choose Snookims and Snookims choose Daddies.

Poor Dears may become real upset if the Bastards treat them with respect, feeling, "He doesn't even care enough to beat me into submission!"

If a Nice Guy divorces the Bitch, chances are very likely that the Nice Guy will choose another Bitch. (A choice, albeit an unconscious choice, but no accident, no coincidence.)

It's all choice.

We get what we intend to get, consciously or unconsciously.

You are responsible for your experience of your spouse. You are the "cause" of your experience.

                                            Stop lying about it.

Take a look at what you're getting out of the relationship
        being what it is
           and start to
        tell the truth about it.

You cannot directly change your spouse,
     so stop trying.

You cannot speed the process of your spouse changing,
     so stop waiting for it to happen.

You don't *need* your spouse,
>   so stop lying about it.

You don't have to look for love
>   if love is where you're coming from.

No relationship will suit you, if you don't feel good about yourself.

In order for the relationship to work, you have to accept the other person exactly the way he or she is right now.

If you find that you are unable to do so, you'd better ask yourself why you're continuing in the relationship.

> Do you really need all the Drama to make your life seem worthwhile?
>
> How long are you going to wait for satisfaction?
>
> How much complaining about your spouse and your relationship are you going to do before you admit that the griping is keeping you stuck and that's how you're getting your jollies?
>
> How long are you going to tell yourself that
>> you "need" the other person?

You don't need anyone.

You might want to *choose* to be with
>   someone.

For a healthy relationship to last, it must come from choice, rather than need.

When you say, "I'm complete.
> I'm a worthy human being
>> and I want to choose to be with you,"
>>> then the relationship will work.

If you say,

"I'm nothing without you.
       I need you to make me happy,"
              chances are it won't work.

To have a relationship work, you need to make an agreement to take total, 100% responsibility to make it work.

      If something stops working in the relationship,
          (and you always know it immediately)
      you'll need:

           to come totally from the truth,

           to get off your position, and

           to give up the Drama.

      That will bring the relationship back to Satisfaction.

You only get from your spouse what you're willing
                      to give to your spouse.

Sometimes all the Drama is just a result of the inability to say, "I love you," and
             "I want you
             to love me."

By not expressing our love directly it becomes thwarted and manifests itself in other ways of being noticed:
                yelling,
                screaming,
                accusing,
                not talking,
                hitting,
                blowing up.

These are all unconscious pleas that say,

"Notice me. Notice me. Love me. Love me. Love me."

Some people feel they need to make war
                to justify making love.

To end or prevent a fight, take a look at what's happening, simply acknowledge what's in it for you, and view the situation from the other person's perspective...
                with love and kindness.

If you find yourself saying,
"You don't love me enough"
look into the mirror and repeat that message.

The true purpose of marriage
is mutual satisfaction –
                not Drama.

Either be willing to give up the Drama or give up the marriage. (An act which in itself could create an incredible new Drama.)
It's far better to simply give up the Drama and save the lawyer's fee.

Giving up the Drama just may allow you to grow and become the "you" you were meant to be,
        with an awareness of self
        that only the unity of marriage
        can provide.

ON FRIENDSHIP

A true friend

> is one who offers you
> another view of reality
> without
> making yours wrong.

The friendship is
like an overlapping bubble of
perception.

It's both the shared reality and the
respect for that portion which isn't.

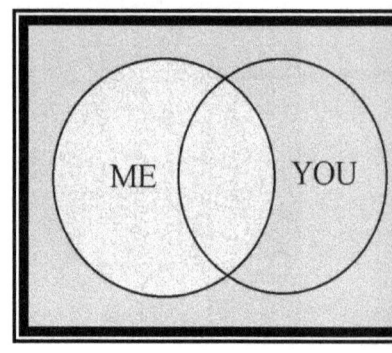

That's what makes it beautiful.

Many of us are afraid to share
ourselves with others,
                      and so we don't have deep friendships.

Sharing is the willingness to put out who we really are
to others and to allow them the same potential.

It's different from
            acting out,
            dramatizing,
            or
            entertaining.

It's letting what's inside come outside.

To allow others to share themselves
       requires a safe space
       without
       concern about judgments,

            right-wrong, or

                stamp collecting
and
            it is the greatest gift of love we can offer.

ON PARENTING

Your kids are you.
>Not just when they're "good,"
>but also when they're "bad."
>They just are the way they are.
>>The rest is all your evaluation.
Take a good look into the mirror your kids provide you.

Children are the most conscious
>most loving
>most accepting
>most happy
>most trusting
>most honest
>most intuitive
>most wise
>>people in the universe.
(How can we not treat them with respect and dignity?)

Notice how you want your kids to behave, and then be it yourself.

Kids are constantly pleading with us to give them responsibility:

"Let me do it."

But because of convenience (or superiority) we keep "helping them," i.e. doing it for them.

We keep them feeling inferior, helpless and not ok, which only reinforces the myth that
> they'll have to find someone to take care of them later in life.

By rescuing, we support the child's Victim notions.

We get involved in the Drama constantly, playing persecutor or rescuer, and then feeling victimized by our own children.

> "Mom, Johnny's hitting me again."

It takes great fortitude not to rescue,
> and to allow others to handle their own problems.

Take a look at what you're doing *for* your kids.

Are you getting them up in the morning,
> and complaining when they're late for breakfast?

Let them get an alarm clock or set their cell phone and take responsibility
> for getting themselves up in the morning.

Are you making certain that they're doing their homework?

That they have done their math problems right?

That they get good grades?

Whose homework is it?

Whose grades are on the report card?

Who's going to take your place when independent
> learning is required?

Are you doing their cooking, setting the table,
doing their wash, driving them around, doing their
dishes, cleaning their rooms, planning their school
activities, defending them at school?

How long are you going to do "for" rather than "with" them?

Of course, age is a factor.

You may have to walk your
two year old across a busy intersection whereas, it's not
appropriate for a fourteen year old.

At some point,
> you have to give up rescuing
>> and allow your children to take responsibility
>>> for their lives.

To let your kids take responsibility
> is to allow them to feel good about themselves.

It's no wonder that so many children
> grow up, leave home, and search for someone
>> to take care of them.
> Then when that doesn't work,
>> they come home and ask for more rescuing.

Why not let your children
take responsibility
> by guiding them, and pointing out what they might
> have done if they failed?

You need to give them the awareness that you have confidence in their ability to solve their own problems and to run their own lives successfully.

The purpose of a family
        is to create a non-judgmental
        atmosphere
        where the individuals can grow
                through love and acceptance.

The family can provide the one safe place where you can truly be yourself and can share yourself with others.

Each member of the family can learn from every other member. No matter how young, children provide us with a blueprint for living.

Christ was accurate
        when He said that we must all
            become as small children to enter the
        kingdom
            of Heaven.

We need to learn from our children,

       the sense of wonder,

       the joy of creating,

         the act of experiencing,

         the freedom of
         emotional expression,

           the wonder and
        beauty of love.

And they need to learn from us how to create a world that will allow them to continue to be who they are and to consciously experience what they're experiencing,

         Right Now.

In order for this to happen, we need to create an environment where the learning can take place ... a trusting, non-threatening environment.

For many parents, the verbal and physical abuse diminishes
when we notice that there are other ways to get close.

We need to become the parents we vowed we would be,
     when we were children.

That would break the cycle that has been repeated for generations.

The ultimate gift you can give your children is to allow them to know who you are, and to allow them the freedom
     to be
     who they are.

ON THERAPY

In therapy,
you'll get well to the extent
that you're willing to tell the truth about how you set up your life the way it is.

Imagine going to a physician with a pain in your arm, and being unwilling to say where you hurt.

    "Doctor, doctor, I'm sick! I hurt!"

        "Where are you experiencing pain?"

        "I won't tell you!"

It's like sitting in the physician's office, hoping to be asked if your arm hurts.

Sound's ridiculous with a physician,
    and yet it happens quite often with therapists.

In order for therapy to work, you have to be willing to face your life, the way you set it up and then be willing to share the truth with your therapist.

Therapy works when it promotes sharing the Truth.

When someone with incredible acts and tapes
> goes to a therapist for "help", it may be a sad joke.

Let's say the client has everything figured out.

> He should be able to put all the pieces together.

> He says, "Doctor what's my problem?"

> There he is asking the therapist the question
> > that only he can answer.

What does the therapist do?

> It depends on whether the therapist is ethical.

It is the height of being unethical

> to keep the client in a Victim position,
> > to buy into the client's lies;
> > > to continue to Rescue week after week,
> >
> > and
> > > to charge money for it.

The client, having no intention of changing, looks for a therapist who will support Victim notions.

> Unwilling to confront the un-comfortableness that significant change will necessitate, the client continues to lie to the therapist and to self.

Eventually, feeling like, "this is getting me nowhere," the client complains bitterly about the loss of money and that the therapist, "didn't help me."
The client continues feeling miserable, only now feels justified in maintaining the problematic behavior, (after all he went for counseling). Then, if all else fails, the search for the magic
            therapist or "cure" continues.

    The joke is on the client and the punch line is, "Guess who's still miserable?"

The Therapist,
    having no intention of really confronting
    the client with the responsibility of having
    created such a life drama, continues to "play it safe"
        through being analytical and detached,
        and by reflecting and listening.

That way the Therapist never once has to ask,

    "Why did you set it up that way?"

    "What are you getting out of it?"

    "When are you going to do something about it?"

The Joke is on the Therapist, because a therapist can't help anyone. And the punch line is "I've tried so hard, and he never followed my advice or did what I told her to do, etc., etc…"

The purpose of therapy is

  to increase the client's level of satisfaction

 by promoting the individual's own potential for problem-solving,

 not to make the individual "feel better" when the good feelings stop with the weekly sessions.

Many therapists
      have "professional" wired up with "passive."

          Some feel that if they can find the
          appropriate label for the behavior
          they won't have to deal with it.

One of the major issues
      confronting the therapeutic relationship

      is promoting conformity,

      to a psychologically fragmented and ill society

      rather than psychological health,
      .

If to be "well" is to be "normal"
      therapy should not be part of the process.

If, as therapists, we teach clients to suppress,

> rather than deal with
>
> or allow the completion of the experience,
>
> we are complicating the process of growth.
>
> Completion cures and it starts with Being the Cause.

Promoting the sharing of all those things the client has been unwilling or unable to share in the past, allows the client control over those aspects of his or her life.

Promoting "twenty questions" is to fall into the trap of the mind and to enhance resistance.

Therapy should encompass a discovery process:

The discovery of self.

The discovery that one's problems are opportunities and abilities.

The discovery that the Truth works.

The discovery that the self is lovable, perfect and worthy.

The discovery that life doesn't have to get bad to get better.

The realization that

> "The Truth is I AM"
>
> And to live life artfully by
> taking total, 100% responsibility
> and Being the Cause.

THE GURU REVISITED

The Truth-Seeker sat confused and frustrated.

After a long pause, he said, "I just don't understand any of this."

"Perhaps you never will," the Guru stated in a knowing, compassionate way.

"You can never understand the Truth.
    You just are the Truth.
        Understanding,
           evaluating,
                and judging are all
                    senseless activities.

            The Truth is You Are.

Your experience is your reality and your reality is a composite of your experience.

We all live in separate realities.

The only one you can ever be sure of is your own.

When something occurs in your experience that you don't like, you can blame something or someone else.

        You can be the effect of your experience
                or you can be the cause of your experience
                and take responsibility for it.

Look at the fact that you've been the cause of your experience all along.

And if there's any change to be made,
                you're the one who is going to have make it happen.

One of the major obstacles for getting your life to work the way you want it to, is your own mind.

Your mind made recordings so you could learn and survive.

Yet your mind is like a plane with no pilot.

It goes unconscious whenever threatened, even though sometimes it's totally inappropriate.

You become unconscious when an association with a past experience is triggered.

This is especially true of negative events.

Because your spiritual nature is one of being completely ethical, every time you act unethically, you pay yourself back by giving up your aliveness and satisfaction.

If you tell lies to yourself,
        you live a life of frustration.
If you tell lies to others,
        you create drama and dissatisfaction.

And yet, you always know the truth because it's your experience. To gain the satisfaction and inner peace you've searched so many years to find,
stop searching and start living.

Realize that satisfaction is a result
  of acceptance,
    of sharing yourself,
      of serving others. and
        of being the cause

Life will continue to flow smoothly when you: give up trying to be someone you're not, stop complaining and lying, establish where you want to go and what you want to have, and then just begin the process, without waiting for it to happen _to_ you, or for someone else to do it _for_ you."

The Truth-Seeker looked up, blinked his eyes, and said: "Yes, I think I'm starting to see it. I understand now... I'm the one who..."

The Truth-Seeker stopped as he watched the Guru become a mirror reflecting his own image.

Knowingly, the Guru smiled and simply disappeared...

FOOTNOTES

p. 93   Matthew 7:12

p. 97   Stephen Karpman. "Fairy Tales and Script Drama Analysis." T.A *Bulletin* 7:26 p. 39-34.

p. 111 Muriel James and Dorothy Jongeward. *Born to Win*. Menlo Park, California: Addison-Wesley.

p. 119 Eric Berne. *Games People Play*. New York: Grove Press.

p. 146 *Webster's Seventh New Collegiate Dictionary*. Springfield, Mass.: G.&.C. Merriam Co.,p.626.

p. 163 Lao Tzu. *The Way of Life According to Lao Tzu*, translated by Witter Bynner. New York: Capricorn Books.

p. 171 David Campbell. *If You Don't Know Where You're Going, You'll Probably End Up Somewhere Else*. Niles, Illinois: Argus Communications.

p. 195 Everett Shostrum and James Kavanaugh, *Between Man and Woman*. Los Angeles: Nash Publishing. Compare with names these authors provide for relationships: Mother/Son, Daddy/Doll, Bitch/Nice Guy, Master/Slave. In the interest of equally negative sexism, these names were altered somewhat for this book. Shostrum and Kavanaugh provide an excellent instrument called the "Love Attraction Inventory."

QUOTES TO LIVE BY...

"Imagination is more important than knowledge."
                                        -Albert Einstein

"Happiness is not in our circumstances, but in ourselves. It is not something we see, like a rainbow, or feel, like the heat of a fire. Happiness is something we are."
                                        -John B. Sheerin

"A man should never be ashamed to say he has been wrong, which is but saying, in other words, that he is wiser today than he was yesterday."
                                        -Alexander Pope

"One who fears, limits his activities. Failure is only the opportunity to more intelligently begin again."
                                        -Henry Ford

"Demanding and rejecting, criticizing and judging, 'righting' and 'wronging' are the sickness of the mind. To be free of distorted perceptions, see the chains of addictive patterns that dominate our consciousness and make our lives a battle. Our perception of others is only your projection of fears and desires for ourselves."
                                        -Kenneth Keyes

"The higher the degree of responsibility, the greater the motivation."
                                        -Kingman Brewster, Jr

"Those who would give up essential liberty to purchase a little temporary safety deserve neither liberty nor safety."
                                        -Benjamin Franklin

"Every individual has a place to fill in the world and is important in some respect, whether he chooses to be so or not."
                                        -Nathaniel Hawthorne

"Without going outside, you may know the whole world. Without looking through the window, you may see the ways of heaven. The farther you go, the less you know."
-Lao Tzu

"No persons are more frequently wrong, than those who will not admit that they are wrong."
-Francois Due de la Rochefoucauld

"The condition of alienation, of being asleep, of being unconscious, of being out of one's mind, is the condition of normal man."
-R.D. Laing

"We have forty million reasons for failure, but not a single excuse."
-Rudyard Kipling

"I am an optimist. It does not seem much use to be anything else."
-Winston Churchill

"Man is never so attached to anything as his own suffering."
-Gurdjieff

"Truth-The Beginning. Peace-The Meaning. Love-The Essence."
-Kriensky

"Face the simple fact before it becomes involved. Solve the small problem before it becomes too big. The most involved fact in the world could have been faced when it was simple. The biggest problem in the world could have been solved when it was small. The simple fact that he finds no problem big is a sane man's prime achievement."
-Lao Tzu

"You can never get enough of what you don't need to make you happy."
-Eric Hoffer

"The statement of our consciousness is the extent to which we joyfully produce results... in our own lives and the lives of others, in the environment of this planet we share."
-Stewart Emery

"Happiness? It is an illusion to think that more comfort means more happiness. Happiness comes of the capacity to feel deeply, to enjoy simply, to think freely, to risk life, to be needed."
-Storm Jameson

"If you ever find happiness by hunting for it, you will find it as the old woman did her lost spectacles – on her nose all the time."
-Josh Billings

"Wealth consists not in having great possessions, but in having few wants."
-Epicurus

"Life is not having and getting, but a being and becoming."
-Matthew Arnold

"In the province of the mind, what one believes to be true, either is true or becomes true within certain limits to be found experientially and experimentally. These limits are further beliefs to be transcended. In the province of the mind, there are no limits."
-John C. Lilly

"Responsibility is a unique concept. It can only reside and inhere in a single individual. You may share it with others, but your portion is not diminished. You may delegate it, but it is still with you. You may disclaim it, but you cannot divest yourself of it."
-Admiral Rickover

"The price of greatness is responsibility." -Winston Churchill

"If you manage people by letting them alone,
Ghosts of the dead shall not haunt you.
Fail to honor people,
They fail to honor you."
-Lao Tzu

"Love joins our present with the past and the future."
-Khalil Gibran

"And only when we are no longer afraid do we begin to live in every experience, painful or joyous; to live in gratitude for every moment, to live abundantly."
-Dorothy Thomson

"The clearer I perceive that which is True, the less reasoning, judging, arguing I can do."
-Angelus Silesius

"It is better to do nothing than to do what is wrong. For whatever you do, you do to yourself. See what is. See what\ is not. Follow the true way. Rise."   -Buddha

"From without, no wonderful effect is wrought within ourselves unless some interior, responding wonder meets it."
-Herman Melville

"The Universe is not to be narrowed down to the limits of the understanding, which has been men's practice up to now ,but the understanding must be stretched and enlarged to take in the image of the universe as it is discovered."
-Francis Bacon

"…it is the soul that thirsts for truth. The intellect only to satiate its fascination."   -Ram Dass

"It's not where you're going, it's where you're coming from."
-Nathaniel Lande

"You become what you behold."   -William Blake

"If you never assume importance, you never lost it."-Lao Tzu

"When at last we understand how we do it to ourselves and create the world we experience, we can live as awakening life."
                                                            -Seneca

"Consciousness is the totality beyond space-time-what may in essence be the real "I". We have come to know that consciousness and energy are one; that all of space-time is constructed by consciousness…Working toward a transformation in consciousness is the only game in town."
                                                            -Bob Toben

"We are what we think. All that we are arises with our thoughts. With our thoughts we make the world."-Buddha

"The individual is responsible for what happens in the future, no matter what has happened in the past… and as long as people are bound by the past, they are not free to respond to the needs and aspirations of others in the present.   -Thomas Harris

"People are always blaming circumstances for what they are .I don't believe in circumstances. The people who get on in this world are the people who get up and look for the circumstances they want, and if they can't find them, make them."
                                                -George Bernhard Shaw

"Something began me and it had no beginning; something will
end me, and it has no end."
                                                    -Carl Sandburg

"Mistaking the false for the true, and the true for the false, you overlook the heart and fill yourself with desire. See the false as false, the true as true, look into your heart. Follow your nature. The fool who knows he is a fool is that much wiser. The fool who thinks he is wise is a fool indeed."
                                                            -Buddha

Recommended Reading

David Augsburger, *Caring Enough to Confront*; Regal.

Richard B. Austin, Jr., *How To Make It With Another Person*; MacMillan.

Richard Bach, *Illusions-the Adventures of a Reluctant Messiah*; Delacorte

Beier & Valens, *People Reading*; Stein Day

Eric Berne, *Games People Play*; Grove Press. *What Do You Say After You Say Hello*? Grove Press.

Nathaniel Branden, *Breaking Free*, Bantam.

Claude M. Bristol, *The Magic of Believing*; Pocket Books.

Harry Browne, *How I Found Freedom in an Unfree World*; Avon.

Richard M. Bucke, *Cosmic Consciousness*; Dutton & Company.

David Campbell, *If You Don't Know Where You're Going, You'll Probably End Up Somewhere Else*, Argus Communications.

Carlos Castandena, *The Teachings of Don Juan*; Pocket Books. *A Separate Reality*; Pocket Books. *Journey to Ixtlan;* Pocket Books. *Tales of Power*, Simon & Schuster.

Ram Dass, *Be Here Now;* Lana Foundation. *The Only Dance There Is*; Anchor Books.

C.D. Deshmukh, *Sparks of the Truth: From the Dissertations of Meher Baba;*

Steward Emery, *Actualizations- You Don't Have to Rehearse to Be Yourself;* Doubleday Dolphin.

Victor E. Frankl, *Man's Search for Meaning;* Pocket Books. Frederick Franck, *The Book of Angelus Silesius*; Vintage Press.

Carl Frederick, est: *Playing the Game the New Way*; Dell.

Erick Fromm, *The Art of Loving*; Bantam. *Escape from Freedom*; Farrar & Reinhart.

Jerry Greenwald, *Be the Person You Were Meant to Be*; Dell.

G.I. Gurdjieff, *All and Everything*; Dutton. *Meetings with Remarkable Men*; Dutton.

Thomas Harris, *I'm OK, You're OK*; Avon.

Robert Hesse, *Journey to the East*; Noonday. *Siddhartha*; New Directions.
Steppenwolf; Holt Rhinehart.

Yoel Hoffman, *The Sound of One Hand*; Basic Books. Aldous Huxley, *Island*; Holt Rhinehart.

James & Jongeward, *Born To Win*; Addison Wesley.

Muriel James, *The OK Boss*; Addison Wesley.

William James, *The Varieties of Religious Experience*; Modern Library.

Arthur Janov, *The Primal Scream*; Putnam.

Ceasar Johnson, *To See a World in a Grain of Sand*; C.R. Gibson Company.

Sidney M. Jourard, *Disclosing Man to Himself*; Van Nostrand-Reinhold *The Transparent Self*; Van Nostrand-Reinhold.

Philip Kapleau, *The Three Pillars of Zen*; Harper & Row.

Sam Keen, *To a Dancing God*; Harper & Row.

Ken Keyes, *Handbook to Higher Consciousness*; Living Love. *Loving Your Body*; Living Love. *Taming Your Mind*; Living Love.

Ken Keyes with Bruce Burkan, *How to Make Your Life Work*; Living Love.

Shelton B. Kopp, *Guru*; Bantam.

J. Krishnamurti, *You Are the World*; Harper & Row. *Commentaries on Living*; Harper & Row. *Education and the Significance of Life*; Harper & Row.

R.D Laing, *The Divided Self*; Pantheon. *The Politics of Experience*; Ballentine. *Knots*; Vintage. *Facts of Life*; Pantheon.

Jess Lair, *I Ain't Much Baby-But I'm All I Got*; Fawcett Crest. *I Ain't Well-But I Sure Am Better*; Fawcett Crest.

Lao Tzu, *Tao Te Ching*; Blackney Translator.

George Leonard, *Simulations of God; The Science of Belief;* Simon & Schuster.

Maxwell Maltz, *Psycho-Cybernetics*: Creative Living for Today; Pocket Books.

Abraham Maslow, *The Farther Reaches of Human Consciousness*; Harper, *Motivation and Personality*; Harper.

Rollo May, *Love and Will*; Norton. *The Courage to Create*; Bantam.

Meher Baba, *God Speaks: the Theme of Creation and its Purpose;* Dodd Mead & Company. *Discourses: Vols 1-4*; Dodd Mead & Company.

Peter McWilliams, *I Love Therefore I Am*; Versemonger Press.

Jeffrey Mishlove, *The Roots of Consciousness*; Random House.

Gerald I. Nierenberg and Henry H. Calero, *Meta-Talk*; Pocket Books.

Ken Olsen, *The Art of Hanging Loose in an Uptight World*; Fawcett Crest.

Robert Ornstein, *The Nature of Human Consciousness*; Viking Press.

P. D. Ouspensky; *In Search of the Miraculous*; Harcourt Brace. *The Psychology of Man's Possible Evolution*; Harcourt Brace. *A New Model of the Universe*; Harcourt Brace. *The Fourth Way*; Knopf.

Joseph C. Pearce, *The Crack in the Cosmic Egg*; Pocket Books.

Fritz Perls, *In and Out the Garbage Pail*; Bantam. *Gestalt Therapy Verbatim*; Bantam.

Frieda Porat with Karen Meyers, *Changing Your Life Style*; Bantam.

Hugh Prather, *I Touch the Earth, the Earth Touches Me*; Real People Press. *Notes To Myself*; Real People Press. Rogers & Stevens, *Person to Person: The Problem of Being*; Real People Press.

Carl Rogers, *On Becoming a Person*; Real People Press.

William Schultz, *Joy: Expanding Human Awareness*; Grove Press.

David Seabury, *The Art of Selfishness*; Cornerstone Library.

Harold Sherman, *How to Take Yourself Apart and Put Yourself Together Again*; Fawcett Crest.

Everett Shostrum, *Man the Manipulator*; Bantam.

Adam Smith, *Powers of the Mind*; Ballantine.

Manuel J. Smith, *When I Say No, I Feel Guilty*; Dial Press.

Claude Steiner, *Scripts People Live*; Grove Press.

David Stuart, *Alan Watts*; Chilton Book Company.

Bob Toben, *Space-Time and Beyond*; Dutton.

Alan Watts, *This Is It*; Random House. *The Book: On the Taboo Against Knowing Who You Are*; Random House. *Psychotherapy East and West*; Ballantine.

About the Author

Dr. G. Michael Durst, developer of the internationally acclaimed seminars, "Management By Responsibility," "Taking P.R.I.D.E." and "Responsible Choices," has extensive professional experience including corporate human resource development, international speaking and management training.

Listed in the *International Directory of Distinguished Leadership* and *Who's Who Internationally*, Dr. Durst was named, "Man of the Year" by the American Biographical Institute.

He has provided responsibility training to over 75,000 men and women from top organizations, such as American Red Cross, B.P., First National Bank, IBM Share, McDonald's, Northwestern Mutual Life, and the African National Congress, to name but a few.

His other book, "Management By Responsibility" is a must read, whether you are a newly-hired manager or an experienced chief executive. It provides extensive background material on individual growth and techniques to change non-productive behavior so organizational and personal goals can be reached. Email ResponsibleLife@aol.com or go to www.ArtofLivingResponsibly.com more information on manuals, books and seminars.

Dr. Durst is also a professional artist. As a psychologist, his paintings are designed to create not only beauty for the beholder, but also a state of relaxation and healing, as testament to the art of living responsibly.

His work is varied—from impressionism to colorful abstracts and "Fractal Visions". However, the one unifying theme in all of his paintings is the emotional link to the heart, which is why he calls his work: "Heartscapes." His exhibitions in New York, Chicago, Cape Town, and the Netherlands have received rave reviews and gained Dr. Durst international renown. His work has won countless First Place awards in international competitions sponsored by Fine Art America. His work can be seen at www.HeartscapePaintings.com

"Fire Lion" by Dr. Michael Durst

www.ingramcontent.com/pod-product-compliance
Lightning Source LLC
Chambersburg PA
CBHW032041150426
43194CB00006B/368